Exp

Tumwater and Lacey

Explore More!

Angie Lea Regensburg

ISBN:
ISBN-10: 1494200554
ISBN-13: 978-1494200558

Dedicated to Braxton
who is eager for adventure,
Nate who has cheered me on,
and my family & friends who encouraged me
to follow my dreams.

Table of Contents

Introduction

Traveling the world can be a marvelous adventure. Filled with experiences; memories captured by camera and by your mind – getting to know local cultures, landmarks and histories.

Olympia and its surrounding communities are no different from the other wonders of the world in that the history is worth knowing. The landmarks are quite breath taking, and the people of past, present and future create a place to treasure. I have seen many places around the world, yet each time I merge from Highway 101 onto I-5 and capture the view of the old brewery on the right, Capitol Lake on my left, and gracing the sky with all its glory – Mt. Rainier, I feel an overwhelming sense of pride. This is truly one of the most beautiful places I have seen on earth. The Olympic Mountains gracefully stand out on the sky line, the tall evergreen trees providing lush beauty all year long, and the number of people who hike, bike, and walk even when it is raining – make this place a jewel to explore.

This book started out my own research to find places that my son and I could go for an hour, an afternoon, or an all day adventure. I found great surprises here and I have visited each location myself. The Olympia area is overflowing with adventures and the rich history of the area has been an added bonus in my research. It was also clear that there were no other books about the area, so this is my gift to you - my fellow Olympia Area Adventurer.

I do love a good adventure and I find that most of the information here is as helpful and informative as I could manage. This is not a book you must read from cover to cover, although I would recommend reading about each place and re-reading before and after your visits. Please remember phone numbers and web site addresses and hours of operation can change, and new construction can sometimes disrupt a trailhead or parks.

My plan for this book is that you USE your copy. If you have a paper copy, write in it. Take notes. Scribble your thoughts about your own adventures. All photographs within this book are my own, but I suggest you take your own pictures. Tape pictures inside. Use it to draw pictures, and keep it with you at all times. If you have an e-copy, load it on your favorite e-reader and take it with you and reference it when needed. Regardless of the format you are using, this book is just the start of your own adventures. Make memories.

This is a book for locals, travelers and newcomers to the area. If you are a native to the area, you might just find a handful of places you have never heard of. Are you new to the area or here for a visit? Use this book to find what others know about the area and to expand your experiences.
I have traveled many places, yet so many places left to explore. To me, the most beautiful place on earth is right here in the Pacific Northwest

Part 1 - Olympia, WA

Located at the southernmost tip of the Puget Sound, Olympia is the Capital of Washington State. Settlers began arriving to the area in 1846 and Olympia was platted in 1850 by Edmund Sylvester. The town was later named to honor the majestic Olympic Mountains that are visible to the north. The climate is mild in the winters and pleasantly warm in the summer. Overflowing with northwest beauty, Olympia is home to an abundance of parks and open spaces. Full of generous and caring people, with award-winning educational systems and eclectic arts – Olympia offers a multitude of adventures.

Artesian Commons

Getting there

415 4th Avenue E, Olympia, WA
Directions: From downtown Olympia, head north on Capitol Way South toward 11th Avenue SE, then turn right onto 4th Avenue East.
Contact: (360)753.8380, olympiawa.gov

Visitor information

Hours: Daily to dusk
Cost: Free
Parking: Free parking

Amenities

* Artesian well

About Artesian Commons

The Artesian Commons offers a .2 acre parking lot and artesian well. The site was designated as a City park on July 23, 2013. The commons currently offers colorful art and activities. Plans include interpretive areas and a food court in spring of 2014.

Recommended planner

Visit the well to fill your reusable water bottle before strolling through downtown for some shopping.

Bigelow House and Museum

Getting there

918 Glass Avenue NE; Olympia, WA
Directions: Take Plum St. SE until it turns into East Bay Dr NE. Turn right on Glass Ave NE.
Contact: (360)753.1215, www.bigelowhouse.org

Visitor information

Hours: May-September Friday, Saturday, Sundays from 12:00-4:00pm
Cost: $3 per adult, $1 under 18. Membership available for free entry.
Parking: Free along the street

Amenities:

- Historic House and Museum guided tours
- Events throughout the year
- Wheel chair accessible

About the Bigelow House and Museum

The Bigelow House and Museum offers 45 minute guided tours May through September three days a week. Tours cover the ground floor of the house, gardens and historic neighborhood.

The house has special significance in the area as it is the oldest home in Olympia, and one of the oldest still standing in the Pacific Northwest. The house was built circa 1860 by pioneer lawyer Daniel R. Bigelow and his school teacher wife Ann Elizabeth White Bigelow. The home is built in a Gothic Revival style and currently sits on more than an acre of the Bigelow family's original land claim.

The house was purchased in 1994 from the Bigelow family by non-profit Bigelow House Preservation Association and opened to the public in 1995, allowing people to experience an authentically preserved Victorian-era family home and more than 140 years of collected furnishings and artifacts.

The museum hosts events throughout the year, offers facilities for group functions and conducts year round tours by appointment. For more information, visit their web site or call.

Recommended planner

Give yourself around 45 minutes to tour Bigelow House Museum, gardens and historic neighborhood.

Bigelow Park

Getting there

1220 Bigelow Street NE; Olympia, WA
Directions: From 4th Ave East, take a left at
Puget St NE. Turn right at Bigelow Ave NE.
Contact: (360)753.8380, olympiawa.gov

Visitor information

Hours: Daily to dusk
Cost: Free
Parking: Free along the street

Amenities:

- 1.9 acres
- Picnic area and shelter
- Restrooms
- Playground
- Basketball
- Public art

About Bigelow Park

Bigelow Park was named for one of Olympia's original pioneer families. Daniel Bigelow was the first territorial Governor of Washington State. Originally part of the historical Bigelow home property, this 1.9 acre park features tall trees, lush grass, and views of the Capitol Dome.

The park features a newer playground with rubber base and whimsical design. Benches and picnic tables are spread beneath the trees offering a shaded or partial sun spot to relax. A covered picnic shelter with restrooms is available at one end of the park near the parking lot. Bigelow Park also offers a basketball hoop and a sidewalk surrounding the park for anyone looking for some activity.

Recommended planner

This park seems to be popular with dog lovers, kids, as well as those who only have an hour-long lunch break. I would recommend bringing a sack lunch and finding a favorite spot and enjoying it under one of the tall trees.

Bigelow Springs

Getting there

930 Bigelow Ave NE; Olympia, WA
Directions: From 4th Ave E, turn left at Quince St NE. Turn right at Bigelow Ave NE. The park is near the bend in the road.
Contact: (360)753.8380, olympiawa.gov

Visitor information

Hours: Daily to dusk
Cost: Free
Parking: Free along the street

Amenities

- 1.3 acres
- Natural spring
- Informational signs

About Bigelow Springs

Nestled in a quiet Olympia neighborhood, this park is a reminder of where our drinking water comes from. Originally part of the Bigelow home property, this site is home to a natural spring. Volunteers from the Sierra Club and other organizations are helping to restore the springs and native vegetation. In the spring, the Volunteers in Parks Program plants naturalized daffodils, which make the park especially enjoyable in the spring.

Informative signs offer a bit of history about the site and Olympia's drinking water. Rock benches near the spring offer a place to rest, or a grassy hill to spread your blanket.

Recommended planner

Come to enjoy the sounds - a babbling spring, birds playing, seagulls in the distance, and the breeze in the trees.

Burfoot Park

Getting there

6927 Boston Harbor Rd. NE; Olympia, WA
Directions: From I-5 take the Port of Olympia exit to Plum Street. Follow Plum Street which becomes East Bay Drive then Boston Harbor Road. Proceed 6 miles. Burfoot County Park will be on your left.
Contact: (360)786.5595, www.co.thurston.wa.us

Visitor information

Hours: Daily 9am to dusk
Cost: Free
Parking: Free inside the park

Amenities

- 1,100 feet of saltwater beach on Budd Inlet
- Nature trails
- Beach access
- Views
- Restroom
- Playground
- Horseshoe pits
- BBQs
- Picnic tables
- Garden
- 3 covered shelters

About Burfoot Park

Burfoot Park is a 50-acre park and offers 1,100 feet of saltwater beachfront on Budd Inlet. Enjoy nature trails, beach access, and views of the State Capital and Olympic Mountains.

Drive into the park from Boston Harbor Road through thetrees and drive the one-way loop around the park to see all that the park has in store for you. The first parking lot you come to provides access to a spacious open area with grass, garden, and picnic tables with barbeques, playground, shelter and restrooms. The climbing toy on the playground is recommended for ages 2 to 5 years of age and there are 4 swings available all with gravel base. There is a restroom accessible at the far end of the open area as well as from other parking areas along the loop.

Drive further around the parameter and find trails meandering off into the trees such as the "Rhododendron Trail", "Forest Shelter Trail," "Beach Trail," "Meadow Shelter," and "Horizon Trail."

The Beach Trail weaves through tall trees, ferns and vines over wooden bridges and staircases. This short trail leads you to Budd Inlet which offers plenty of opportunity for beach adventure. On a sunny day, the beach provides views of the State Capital, Olympic Mountains and boats.

Burfoot Park offers three covered shelters. The Main Shelter is located in the middle of the park and offers the largest space with large barbecue grill, electrical outlet and four picnic tables offering seating capacity for 32-40 people. The Meadow Shelter is southwest of the Main Shelter and offers a secluded meadow. This shelter offers barbecue grill and 3 picnic tables with a seating capacity of 24-30 people. The third shelter; the Forest Shelter, is located west of the main shelter in a wooded area and opposite the restrooms. The Forest Shelter offers one large picnic table and barbeque grill with a seating capacity of 24-30 people.

Recommended planner

The possibilities are endless at Burfoot Park. Come for a family get together in one of the 3 covered shelters, bring your dog for a walk (leash laws apply), or bring a Frisbee down to the beach and enjoy the wide open areas for an afternoon of fun. Whatever you choose, Burfoot Park surely has enough to come back repeatedly.

Burri

Getting there

2415 Burbank Ave NW, Olympia, WA
Directions: Head north on Capitol Way South toward 11th Avenue SE, turn left onto Amanda Smith Way SW, turn right onto Columbia St SW, turn left onto 5th Ave SW, at the traffic circle, take the 2nd exit onto Olympic Way, at the traffic circle, take the 2nd exit onto Harrison Ave NW, turn right onto Division St NW, turn left onto Burnbank Ave NW. The destination will be on the left.
Contact: (360)753.8380, olympiawa.gov

Visitor information

Hours: Daily to dusk
Cost: Free
Parking: Free parking

Amenities

- 2.32 acres
- Grass meadow
- Swing set
- Half-court basketball
- Short trail

About Burri

Burri park is a 2.32 acre park that is adjacent to the Deer Run Apartments. Originally, the park was surveyed in 1999; an interim management plan was set in motion in 2007. The park received its name in 2009 in recognition of Jim Burri who founded and served as president of the Burbank Neighborhood Association. The park offers native vegetation and a swing set.

Capitol Lake

Getting there

14th and Capitol Way; Olympia, WA
Directions: From I-5, take exit 105 and follow signs to the Port of Olympia. Follow Plum Street. Take a left on Fifth Street. Continue on Fifth Street to the north end of Capitol Lake. From south of Olympia, take I-5 to exit 104 and turn onto Deschutes Parkway. Continue on Deschutes Parkway under I-5 to the south end of Capitol Lake
Contact: (360)753.8380, olympiawa.gov

Visitor information

Hours: Daily to dusk
Cost: Free
Parking: Limited free parking

Amenities

- Lake
- Views
- Walking path
- Benches
- Grass
- Boating

About Capitol Lake

Capitol Lake is situated in downtown Olympia. Capitol Lake was formed by a dam where the fresh water Deschutes River empties into salt water of Budd Inlet. From the top of the dam, salmon can be seen making their way upstream during spawning season starting mid-August. A paved path around the parameter of Capitol Lake offers opportunity for walkers, runners, and bikers. The path connects Marathon Park to Heritage Park and the Capitol Lake Interpretive Center. There is also a path from the paved trail up the hill that takes you to the Washington State Capitol Campus.

An annual event called Capitol Lakefair is always a treat for all ages. Lakefair provides arts and crafts booths, food booths, boat races, car shows, parade, fireworks, live entertainment, volleyball tournaments, carnival rides and so much more! For information on Lakefair, visit www.lakefair.org.

Recommended planner

If you have a full day, take a walk around the lake and read the plaques for Washington cities along the way. Stop for a rest on a bench at Heritage Park for a view of the Capitol Building, and then make your way up the hill to the Washington State Capitol Campus for a view of the city.

Capitol Lake Interpretive Center

Getting there

Deschutes Parkway; Olympia, WA
Directions: From downtown, follow 5th Avenue
to Deschutes Parkway and follow to the southern
part of Capitol Lake.
Contact: (360)902.8881

Visitor information

Hours: Daily to dusk
Cost: Free
Parking: Free along Deschutes Parkway

Amenities

- Floating dock
- Restrooms
- Trail
- Pet station
- Views
- Wildlife

About Capitol Lake Interpretive Center

One of 3 state managed parks on the shores of Capitol Lake, the Capitol Lake Interpretive Center provides opportunity for viewing wildlife, Capitol Lake and the Legislative Building.

This small park has a restroom, pet station, and a floating dock.

Recommended planner

This would be a great starter spot, middle spot or end spot for a walk or bike ride around the lake any time of year.

Chambers Lake Park

Getting there

4808 Herman Road SE, Olympia, WA
Directions: From I-5 north, take exit 107 for Pacific Avenue, turn right onto Pacific Avenue SE, turn right on Fones Road SE, at the traffic circle, take the 1st exit onto 18th Avenue SE/Fones Road SE, at the traffic circle, take the 3rd exit onto Hoffman Road SE, turn left onto 27th Avenue SE, continue onto Wiggins Road SE, turn left onto Herman Road SE, the destination will be on the left.
Contact: (360)753.8380, olympiawa.gov

Visitor information

Hours: Daily to dusk
Cost: Free
Parking: Free parking

Amenities

- 46.2 acres of undeveloped parkland
- Forested wetlands
- Upland forest
- Large open field

About Chambers Lake Park

Chambers Lake Park was established in 2008 and is adjacent to Chambers Lake and the Chehalis-Western Trail.

Columbus Park at Black Lake

Getting there

5700 Black Lake Blvd SW #62; Olympia, WA
Directions: From US-101, take Black Lake Blvd exit to West Olympia. Turn left on Black Lake Blvd SW. It is located on the left and clearly marked with signs.
Contact: (360)786.9460, www.columbuspark.net

Visitor information

Hours: Daily to dusk
Cost: $5 day use fee (call to verify current rate)
Parking: Free with day use pass

Amenities:

* Day use area
* Beach access
* Swimming (no lifeguard)
* Amphitheater

-
- Open grass
- Picnic tables
- Boat launch
- Facility rentals
- Camping
- Fishing

- Playground
- Horseshoe pits
- Volleyball pits
- Restrooms
- Showers

About Columbus Park at Black Lake

Columbus Park has been in operation since 1926, providing year round residence and summer fun. Though there is a small day use fee, Columbus Park has a lot to offer.

The park offers day use area, beach access, enormous amphitheater, open grass area, picnic areas, and kitchens. A fishing area, playground, restrooms, showers, horseshoe and volleyball pits are also offered. There is an area for swimming (no lifeguard), with large roped off area for younger swimmers and a swim dock for older swimmers. Camping is available (30 campsites located in shade surrounded by trees with year round creek flowing through them), RV sites, sites with electricity and water.

Recommended planner

Because there is a small fee associated with entering the park, it is recommended that you make the most of your time in the park. Plan a full day at the park and remember to bring cooler, towels, swim suits and plenty of sun block.

Cooper Crest Open Space

Getting there

3600 20th Avenue NW
Directions: From I-5 south, take exit 104 to merge onto US-101 north, take the Black Lake Blvd exit toward West Olympia. Keep right at the fork, follow signs for West Olympia and merge onto Black Lake Blvd SW. Turn left onto Cooper Point Road SW, turn left onto 20th Avenue NW. The destination will be on your right.
Contact: (360)753.8380, olympiawa.gov

Visitor information

Hours: Daily to dusk
Cost: Free
Parking: No parking at either trailhead

Amenities

* 13.37 acres
* Forested open space
* Hiking trail

About Cooper Crest Open Space

Purchased in 2003, Cooper Crest Open Space offers an out-and-back trail that is approximately ¼ mile in length. The trailhead is located on 20th Avenue NE, with a second trail connection from the Cooper Crest subdivision.

Decatur Woods Park

Getting there

1015 Decatur Street SW; Olympia, WA
Directions: From west Olympia, take 9th Avenue Southwest from Black Lake Blvd. Turn right on Decatur Street. The park is one block down Decatur at the intersection of 10th Avenue.
Contact: (360)753.8380, olympiawa.gov

Visitor information

Hours: Daily to dusk
Cost: Free
Parking: Free along the street

Amenities:

- 6.27 acres
- Picnic area
- Picnic tables
- Nature trails

- Restrooms
- Playground
- Open grass
- Public art

About Decatur Woods Park

Located off Decatur Street in Olympia, this newly established park opened in September 2004. The park has a fence that separates most of one side to protect from Decatur Street. It is well maintained and offers open grass and a covered picnic area with electric and water for public use.

Restrooms, water fountain and bike racks are located close to the road. The park offers paved trails along Decatur Street as well as a paved loop through Douglas fir trees. Public Art designed by Olympia artist Nikki McClure can be found near the loop trail into the woods.

Decatur Woods Park offers two separate Timberform Pipeline playgrounds on a rubber base with fun designs. One big toy is recommended for ages 3-5 years and offers a steering wheel, short slide and short climbing area. The second big toy is recommended for ages 5-12 and offers tall climbs, twisty slide and bridges.

Pets at Decatur Woods Park must be kept on a leash. A pet station is available which offers bags for cleaning pet waste.

Recommended planner

Decatur Woods Park is a beautiful neighborhood park that should surely be used by the area residents. If you are from outside the neighborhood or area, I recommend taking a trip to bask in the openness of the park. Enjoy the sun, let the kids explore the playground, and do not forget the sun block because there is very little shade here.

East Bay Waterfront

Getting there

313 East Bay Drive NE; Olympia, WA
Directions: From downtown, turn North on Plum Street which turns into East Bay Drive.
Contact: (360)753.8380, olympiawa.gov

Visitor information

Hours: Daily
Cost: Free
Parking: Free parking along nearby streets

Amenities

- 1.86 acres
- Picnic areas
- Waterfront
- Viewing platform

About East Bay Waterfront

Small Waterfront Park offers interpretive signs and views of East Bay. This location makes a nice rest stop for walkers and joggers. Beautiful view of the Cascade Mountains, marina and boats can be seen from a viewing platform and paved path along the waterfront.

Recommended Planner

Start at the Farmers Market on a clear morning and take a walk to this waterfront park and enjoy the beauty of Olympia.

Ellis Cove Trail

Getting there

2600 East Bay Drive NE; Olympia, WA
(Inside Priest Point Park)
Directions: From downtown Olympia, follow East
Bay Drive north. Enter Priest Point Park on your
right. Once inside the park, follow around and
back over East Bay drive into the west side of the
park. The trail head is near the point.
Contact: (360)753.8380, olympiawa.gov

Visitor information

Hours: Daily to dusk
Cost: Free

Parking: Free near the trail head inside Priest Point Park

Amenities

- Nature trail
- Benches
- Informational signs
- Viewpoints
- Beach access
- Shade / Sun

About Ellis Cove Trail

Ellis Cove Trail is a 3-mile loop trail located inside Priest Point Park in Olympia. The trail offers lush forested paths, serene views, educational signs, and beach access.

The original trail was developed in 1980 and after heavy use, the deteriorated trail required considerable repair. In 1988 trail renovation involved restoration of the trail, new trail development, and construction of new bridges.

On your walk through lush forest you will see tall trees, hanging moss, skunk cabbage, views of the water, wooden bridges, and stairs climbing up hills. There are six interpretive stations describing the parks cultural history, wildlife and other natural resources.

A brochure is available at the trail head which contains a map and an informational guide for your walk.

Recommended Planner

Bring sturdy footwear, camera, binoculars and a book on Northwest plants or birds. Grab a map at the trail head or off the parks and recreation web site. Take some extra time to hike out to the beach to enjoy the views of the Capitol Building and water. Several large driftwood pieces resting on the shore of the beach make the perfect spot for a picnic lunch.

Evergreen Park

Getting there

1445 Evergreen Park Drive SW, Olympia WA
Directions: From I-5 south, take exit 104 to merge onto US-101 north. Take the Cooper Point Road exit, keep right at the fork and follow signs for Crosby Boulevard. Turn right onto Cooper Point Road SW, take the first right onto Evergreen Park Drive SW. The destination will be on the right.
Contact: (360)753.8380, olympiawa.gov

Visitor information

Hours: Daily to dusk
Cost: Free
Parking: Free parking

Amenities

- 4 acres
- Picnic tables
- Swing set
- Bocce court
- Rock trail loop
- Edible landscaping

About Evergreen Park

Evergreen Park is a neighborhood park located off Evergreen Park Drive SW. The park offers a walking loop trail through forest and meadow, as well as picnic tables and swings.

Farmers Market

Getting there

700 Capitol Way N. Olympia, WA
Directions: From I-5, take exit 105A to City Center, turn right on Capitol Way, follow north through downtown Olympia toward the waterfront.
Contact: (360)352.9096, www.farmers-market.org

Visitor information

Hours: April-October: Thur-Sun 10am – 3pm
November-December: Sa-Su 10am – 3pm
Cost: Free entertainment, items for purchase.
Parking: Free 2 hour parking located in the market lots.

Amenities:

- Locally grown fresh fruits and vegetables
- Homemade foods
- Farm fresh meat and dairy items
- One of a kind locally made arts and crafts
- Top quality plants
- Stage with live entertainment
- Demonstration garden
- Restrooms
- ATM
- Food stands

About the Farmers Market

The Olympia Farmers Market is a great way to buy locally grown foods and handmade items. Local farmers, artisans, and community members come together to make their products available to the residents of the community.

Started in 1973, the original market began on the shores of Capitol Lake as a project of the Retired Senior Volunteer Program. The goal of the market was to promote good nutrition for seniors.

In 1975, the market moved to Plum Street where it stayed for 8 years. The current market location was established in the 1980s, where it remains to this day. The existing structures were completed in 1996 providing a larger market area with covered areas for food vendors, a stage, a demonstration garden and restrooms.

Recommended planner

I recommend frequenting the market for fresh food items weekly. Call or check the web site for event information and current operating hours.

Friendly Grove Park

Getting there

2316 Friendly Grove Road NE; Olympia, WA
Directions: From 4th Avenue E, turn left on Puget St NE. Turn right at San Francisco Ave NE. Make a left at Bethel St NE then right at Miller Ave NE. Turn left at Friendly Grove Rd. NE.
Contact: (360)753.8380, olympiawa.gov

Visitor information

Hours: Daily to dusk
Cost: Free
Parking: Free in lot

Amenities:

- 14.5 acres
- Picnic areas
- Shelter
- Restroom
- Playground
- Basketball

- Tennis
- Novice skate court
- Paved loop trail
- Public art

About Friendly Grove Park

Friendly Grove Park is one of Olympia's newest parks. This beautifully landscaped park is located in the Friendly Grove neighborhood. Once home to strawberry fields and dairy cows, Friendly Grove now has plenty of space for activity for all.

The park offers large open grass areas, picnic shelter with tables and public restrooms. A playground with rubber base, swings, slides and a wooden climbing area provide fun for young members of the community. The park also offers a paved loop trail around the park, and sports courts for the active members of the community.

Friendly Grove Park has a paved skate court area with rails for novice skaters.

A pet station is available with clean up bags and pet guidelines.

Recommended Planner

Whatever you fancy, this park overflows with possibilities. Bring the little ones to ride their bikes on the paved trail that winds around the park. Bring your skateboard and practice your newest moves. Bring a basketball or tennis racquet and share a game with a friend. Or simply bring a blanket to relax in the grass and take in the beauty this park has to offer.

Frye Cove County Park

Getting there

4000 NW 61st Ave; Olympia, WA
Directions: From I-5 in Olympia, north or southbound, take Exit 104 (US north, Aberdeen). Stay on US 101 toward Shelton. Take the Steamboat Island Rd Exit. Go north on Steamboat Island Rd NW about 5.8 miles and turn right onto Young Road NW. Proceed about 2 miles, turn left on 61st Ave NW into Frye Cove County Park.
Contact: (360)786.5595, www.co.thurston.wa.us

Visitor information

Hours: Daily to dusk
Cost: Free
Parking: Free parking in the park

Amenities

- 67 acres
- Nature trails
- Views
- Beach access

About Frye Cove County Park

Frye Cove Park is located west of Olympia on Steamboat Island. This 64 acre park offers over 2 miles of trails, outstanding views of Mt. Rainier and 1400 feet of saltwater beach on Eld Inlet.

Frye Cove is known to be the perfect setting for weddings, nature walks and shellfish gathering.

Recommended Planner

Frye Cove is a bit of a drive but a great place to come for a hike through towering trees and to catch breathtaking views and enjoy the peaceful sounds of nature.

Garfield Nature Trail

Getting there

620 Rogers Street NW or 701 West Bay Drive NW; Olympia, WA

Directions: To West Bay Drive NW: Take US 101 to Black lake Blvd exit. Turn left at Black Lake Blvd and continue as it turns into Division St. NW. Turn right at Harrison Ave NW and then at the roundabout follow it onto West Bay Drive NW.

To Rogers Street: Take US 101 to Black lake Blvd exit. Turn left at Black Lake Blvd and continue as it turns into Division St. NW. Turn right at Conger Ave NW and right at Rogers St NW.

Contact: (360)753.8380, olympiawa.gov

Visitor information

Hours: Daily to dusk
Cost: Free
Parking: Free on neighboring streets

Amenities

- 7.41 acres
- Nature trail
- Creek

About Garfield Nature Trail

Garfield Nature Trail meanders through a five-acre ravine from West Bay Drive to North Rogers street. A creek at the base of the trail carries runoff water from the surrounding area.

Grass Lake Refuge

Getting there

3133 14th Ave NW; Olympia, WA
Directions: From Mud Bay Road turn onto
Kaiser Road NW. There is a chain fence on the
right that gives access to the Refuge.
Contact: (360)753.8380, olympiawa.gov

Visitor information

Hours: Daily to dusk
Cost: Free
Parking: Free at entrance

Amenities

- Nature trail
- Views

About Grass Lake Refuge

At the entrance of the park, through a chain fence, a sign shows you a map of the refuge. A short walk takes you onto a narrow path between trees. This is a loop trail and takes about 30 minutes to walk. In summer your only glimpse of water can be found at the start of the trail before the loop where you can catch a view of Lake Louise.

The Grass Lake Refuge was acquired in the late 1980s after property owners, citizen groups and the Olympia City Council gave steady vigil against land developers. In 1989 the Friends of Grass Lake acquired the refuge for 1.8 million dollars. The Refuge is approximately 165 acres of wetlands, coniferous forest, and meadows. The area is home to over 200 species of plants and 98 species of birds. It is a seasonal wetland that fills up in fall and winter and almost completely empties during summer.

The future use of this site will be limited to interpretive nature trails and environmental education.

Recommended planner

Great for a calm morning walk, bird watching, or photography.

Griffin Athletic Fields

Getting there

6924 41st Ave NW; Olympia, WA
Directions: From I-5 South, take US-101 N exit 104 to Aberdeen Port Angeles, then continue to follow 101 towards Shelton. Turn right at Oyster Bay Rd NW; turn right at 41st Ave NW. The fields are on your left.
Contact: (360)786.5595, www.co.thurston.wa.us

Visitor information

Hours: Daily to dusk
Cost: Free
Parking: Free in lot

Amenities

- 2 soccer / football fields
- 1 softball / baseball field

About Griffin Athletic Fields

Griffin Athletic Fields were completed in spring of 2005. This site has 3 fields for soccer, football, softball and baseball.

Harry Fain's Legion Park

Getting there

300 5th Avenue SW; Olympia, WA
Directions: From downtown Olympia, Follow
Eastside St. South. Turn left on 20th Avenue.
The park is immediately on your right.
Contact: (360)753.8380, olympiawa.gov

Visitor information

Hours: Daily to dusk
Cost: Free
Parking: Free limited parking along 20th Avenue

Amenities

- 2.3 acres
- Playground
- Picnic area
- Picnic tables
- Nature trails

About Harry Fain's Legion Park

Legion Park is a quaint woodsy park that was donated to the city by Harry Fain in 1933. This 2.3 acre park was developed in 1987 by the Parks, Arts and Recreation Department and neighborhood residents.

Recommended Planner

Legion Park is great spot on a hot day. Enjoy tall trees and shade in the afternoon. Continue your adventure at nearby Watershed Park.

Heritage Park (at Capitol Lake)

Getting there

5th Avenue; Olympia, WA
Directions: From I-5 south take the State Capitol
/ City Center / Port of Olympia exit (#105).
Continue on 14th Ave SE and turn right at Capitol
Way S. Turn left on 5th Avenue.
Contact: (360)753.8380, Dept of General
Admission: (360)902.0944, olympiawa.gov

Visitor information

Hours: Daily to dusk
Cost: Free
Parking: Free limited 2 hour parking 5am – 11pm
in the lot. Metered parking along nearby streets
also available.

Amenities

- 24 acres
- Benches
- Walking path
- At Capitol Lake
- Close to Downtown
- Views

About Heritage Park

Heritage Park is a beautiful park located in
downtown Olympia. This 24 acre park is state
owned and borders northern Capitol Lake. The
park offers spectacular views of the Capitol
Building.

The construction of the park completes a master plan of the Capitol Campus from 1911 that was created by architects Walter Wilder and Harry White who designed the Legislative Building. The vision for the park was to physically and visually connect the State Capitol to downtown Olympia, Puget Sound and the Olympic Mountains.

Capitol Lake Fair is hosted annually at Heritage Park.

Recommended Planner

Whether lounging in the grass on a sunny afternoon, strolling around the walking path, or enjoying one of the events hosted at Heritage Park, you are sure to find plenty of adventure here.

Heritage Park Fountain

Getting there

300 5th Avenue SW; Olympia, WA
Directions: From I-5 South take the State Capitol / City Center / Port of Olympia exit (#105). Continue on 14th Ave SE and turn right at Capitol Way S. Turn left on 5th Avenue.
Contact: (360)753.8380, olympiawa.gov

Visitor information

Hours: June-September
Thursday-Tuesday
10am-1:30pm
3:30pm-9:30pm

October-May
Thursday-Tuesday
10am-9:30pm
Cost: Free
Parking: Free and Metered Parking on nearby streets

Amenities

- 1.11 acres
- Picnic area
- Fountain for splashing

About Heritage Park Fountain

Purchased in 1996, this 1.11-acre downtown park has a beautifully playful fountain for wading and splashing. The fountain is made up of a circular display of waterjets that spray water toward the sky with a pop and a shower of water.

The fountain closes twice a day to maintain the water quality. The water is filtered through a bromine system to protect public health. On Wednesdays, the fountain is closed to change the water and undergo routine maintenance.

A grassy area surrounds the fountain and in the summer months, vendors might sell snow cones and laughter can be heard as small children and even adults delight in the sprays from the fountain.

Recommended Planner

Perfect for a splash on a sunny afternoon or watching the lights and fountains on a warm evening.

Kennydell Athletic Fields

Getting there

6631 Fairview Road SW, Olympia, WA
Directions: From I-5 South: Take US-101 Exit 104 toward Aberdeen/Port Angeles. Take the exit toward Black Lake. Turn left onto Black Lake Blvd SW. Turn left onto Black Lake-Belmore Rd SW. Turn right onto 66TH Ave SW. Take the 1st left onto Fairview Rd SW. Kenneydell Park is on the right.
Contact: (360)786.5595, www.co.thurston.wa.us

Visitor information

Hours: Daily to dusk
Cost: Free
Parking: Free in lot

Amenities:

- Baseball field
- Soccer field

About Kennydell Athletic Fields

Completed in September 2003, Kenneydell Athletic Fields offer one baseball field and one soccer field.

Recommended Planner

This is an excellent place to play or watch local sports.

Kennydell Park

Getting there

6745 SW Fairview Rd; Olympia, WA
Directions: Take Highway 101 off I-5. Exit onto Black Lake Boulevard southbound. Proceed approximately 2 miles, then turn left onto the Black Lake-Belmore Road. Follow the Black Lake-Belmore Road approximately 2 miles. Turn right onto 66th. At the sharp curve to the left, 66th will become known as Fairview Road. Kenneydell County Park entrance is 600 feet after the curve on the right.
Contact: (360)786.5595, www.co.thurston.wa.us

Visitor information

Hours: Daily to dusk
Cost: Free
Parking: Free in lot

Amenities:

- 41 acres
- 1,000 feet freshwater waterfront
- Swim area
- Beach
- Picnic shelters

About Kennydell Park

This 41 acre Thurston County Park features 1,000 feet of freshwater waterfront, a swim area and beach on Black Lake. The park offers three covered shelters (The Pioneer Shelter, The Ridge Shelter, The Creekside Shelter) that provide a large barbecue grill and three picnic tables each that seat 24-30 people.

A lodge can be reserved up to one year in advance. The lodge has capacity for 49 people; offers heated meeting area, covered porches, kitchen, and fireplace.

Kettle View Park

Getting there

1250 Eagle Bend Drive SE
Directions: From I-5 south, take exit 105 toward
State Capitol/City Center/Port of Olympia. Take
exit 105B toward Port of Olympia, turn left onto
Henderson Blvd SE, at the traffic circle, continue
straight to stay on Henderson Blvd SE. Turn right
onto Briggs Drive SE, turn right onto Dogwood
Drive SE, turn right onto Eagle Bend Drive SE.
Contact: (360)753.8380, olympiawa.gov

Visitor information

Hours: Daily to dusk
Cost: Free
Parking: Free parking

Amenities

- Playground
- Swings
- Tennis court
- ¼ mile paved loop trail
- 1.8 acre play field
- Restroom
- Picnic shelter

About Kettle View Park

Kettle View Park was purchased in 2007 and
named in 2011 for the parks proximity to several
glacial kettles. The park opened on September
23, 2011. Future plans include community
gardens, basketball court, skate node and open
areas.

Lake Lucinda Community Park

Getting there

8701 Lake Lucinda Dr.; Olympia, WA
Directions: From I-5 south, take the US-101 N exit 104 to Aberdeen/Port Angeles. Take the Black Lake Blvd Exit to West Olympia. Turn Left at Black Lake Blvd SW and continue on 62nd Ave SW. Turn left at Delphi Rd SW. Turn Right at Waddell Creek Rd SW. Turn left at Lake Lucinda Dr SW.

Visitor information

Hours: Daily to dusk
Cost: Free
Parking: Free along Lake Lucinda Dr

Amenities

- Ball field
- Basketball
- Tennis court
- Club house
- BBQ
- Playground

About Lake Lucinda Community Park

A cozy neighborhood park nestled in the Lake Lucinda Community. Park boasts an abundance of open grass area and plenty of opportunity for activity and adventure. This is a park for the members of Lake Lucinda Community.

Recommended planner

A wonderful neighborhood park to run with kids, climb on the playground or enjoy a casual game of ball.

LBA Park

Getting there

333 Morse-Merryman Rd. SE or 3500 Amhurst St. SE; Olympia, WA

Directions: (To Amhurst St SE): From I-5 South, take the Sleater Kinny Rd. S exit 108. Bear right onto the Sleater Kinney Rd. SE ramp. Turn right at 14th Ave SE. Bear left at Elizabeth St. SE. Bear right at 18th Ave. SE. Turn left at Hoffman Rd SE. Turn right at 30th Ave SE.

Contact: (360)753.8380, olympiawa.gov

Visitor information

Hours: Daily to dusk
Cost: Free
Parking: Free inside the park

Amenities

- 22.61 acres
- Picnic areas
- Picnic tables
- Picnic shelters
- Playground
- Basketball
- Tennis
- Athletic fields
- Running track
- Restrooms
- Concessions

About LBA Park

LBA Park in Olympia was established in 1974 by the Little Baseball Association (LBA). The park offers picnic facilities, playground, basketball, tennis, athletic fields, running track, restrooms and a concession stand.

Priority of field scheduling is given to the Little Baseball Association for programs and activities.

Lions Park

Getting there

800 Wilson Street SE; Olympia, WA
Directions: From I-5 South take Pacific Ave SE exit 107. Turn right at Pacific Ave SE. Turn left at Boulevard Rd SE. Turn right at 7th Ave SE. Turn left at Wilson St. SE.
Contact: (360)753.8380, olympiawa.gov

Visitor information

Hours: Daily to dusk
Cost: Free
Parking: Free parking off Fredrick Street or around perimeter of park

Amenities

- 3.72 acres
- Picnic area
- Restrooms

- Playground
- Basketball
- Tennis
- Horseshoe pits
- Play field
- Public art

About Lions Park

Dedicated in 1946, Lions Park is a partnership between the Eastside Neighborhood Association and the Olympia Lions Service Club. Lions Park is a wonderful family park, with plenty of open space lined with trees, an older wooden playground that gets sun and shade, swing set, picnic facilities, and restrooms.

Recommended Planner

Perfect place to play your favorite games or even fly a kite, Lions Park has a bit for everyone. For the little ones, it seems a great deal of fun can be had jumping from stone to stone on the rock art in the park.

Madison Scenic Park

Getting there

1600 10th Avenue SE; Olympia, WA
Directions: From I-5 South, take the Pacific Ave
SE exit 107 and turn right onto Pacific Ave SE.
Bear left at State Ave NE. Turn left at Fir St NE
and continue on Fir St SE. Turn right at 10th Ave
SE.
Contact: (360)753.8380, olympiawa.gov

Visitor information

Hours: Daily to dusk
Cost: Free
Parking: Free parking in small lot on 10th
Avenue SE

Amenities:

- 2.21 acres
- Walking paths
- Benches
- Wildflowers
- Views

About Madison Scenic Park

At first glance, this park seems to be a forgotten spot. Climb the grassy hill and you can sit in a patch of forget-me-nots or on a hillside bench to enjoy a spectacular view of the Capitol Building and Black Hills. Short trees boarder the hill but don't block the view. Benches provide seating and some trails wind their way along the hill. A ball field can be seen at the lower level of the park.

Dedicated in 1989, Madison Scenic Park is owned by the Olympia School district and is maintained by the Eastside Neighborhood Association and the Olympia Parks, Arts & Recreation department.

Recommended planner

Climb the short hill with a camera, journal or sketchbook and take it all in!

Marathon Park

Getting there

Deschutes Parkway, Olympia, WA.
Directions: Located along Deschutes Parkway along Capitol Lake

Visitor information

Hours: 5:00 AM – 11:00 PM
Cost: Free
Parking: Limited free parking in lot, additional parking along road

Amenities

- 2.25 acre waterfront park
- Nature trail
- Informative signs
- Picnic Tables
- Restrooms
- Drinking Fountain

About Marathon Park

Part of the Washington State Capitol Campus, Marathon Park was named in honor of the first U.S. Women's Olympic Marathon Trials. These trials took place in Olympia on May 12, 1984. The 2.25 acre park sits along the Capitol Lake shoreline and offers visitors lush green grass, scattered trees for shade and beautiful views of the lake. Many locals start here for a run or walk around the lake.

Margaret McKenny Park

Getting there

3111 21st Avenue SE, Olympia, WA
Directions: From Pacific Ave SE, turn right onto Fones Road SE, at the roundabout, take the first exit onto 18th Ave SE, at the roundabout, take second exit. Turn left onto Craig Rd SE, turn right onto 21st Avenue SE.
Contact: (360)753.8380, olympiawa.gov

Visitor information

Hours: Daily to dusk
Cost: Free
Parking: Free parking

Amenities

- 4.16 acres
- Picnic tables
- Swing set
- Basketball
- Loop trail

About Margaret McKenny Park

Margaret McKenny park was named for Olympia resident Margaret McKenny. Ms. McKenny distributed a petition to save Watershed Park from private development in 1955. The park today has a loop trail through forest, open grassy meadow and picnic tables.

Recommended planner

Stop in for a quick stroll along the crushed rock trail and finish off with some basketball.

McGrath Woods Park

Getting there

2300 Cain Road SE, Olympia, WA
Directions: From I-5 south, take exit 105 toward the Port of Olympia. Keep straight onto East Bay Dr, keep straight onto Plum St SE, turn right onto Pear St SE. Turn right onto Union Ave SE, then right onto Eastside St SE. The road name changes to 22nd Ave SE. Turn right onto Cain Rd.
Contact: (360)753.8380, olympiawa.gov

Visitor information

Hours: Daily to dusk
Cost: Free
Parking: Free parking

Amenities

- 4 acres
- Picnic tables
- Grass meadow
- Swings
- Crushed rock loop trail

About McGrath Woods Park

McGrath Woods Park is a 4-acre park that was purchased as a future neighborhood park. Interim use plan was approved in 2007 and improvements were made to the park in 2009.

Recommended planner

Walk the rock loop trail and be sure to swing on the swing set.

McLane Creek

Getting there

Delphi Road; Olympia, WA
Directions: From Olympia – Take the Evergreen
State College exit from northbound Hwy 101.
Take the Mud Bay Exit. Turn left at the stop sign
and left again on Delphi Road. At 3.4 miles, turn
right at the DNR McLane Creed Nature Trail sign.
Contact: (360)577.2025, www.dnr.wa.gov

Visitor information

Hours: Daily to 8pm
Cost: Free
Parking: Free parking in lo.

Amenities

- Nature trail
- Vault toilets
- Viewing platforms
- Wetland
- Informative signs

About McLane Creek

Managed by the Department of Natural Resources, the McLane Creek Nature Trail offers nature trails through Capitol State Forest and area marshlands. The trail follows an old railroad grade where old growth logs were once taken to Puget Sound on steam locomotives. Now the trail offers boardwalks, dirt and gravel paths and winding trails through evergreen and deciduous woods. A beaver pond and marsh viewing platforms offer views and interpretive signs describe ecology and managed forestry practices.

The main trail is over 1 mile in distance, however a shorter loop branches off and about half the distance.

Leash and scoop laws apply to pets.

Recommended planner

One of our favorite walking trails in the area; it is a nice little hike and plenty of wildlife to see along the way. Another great walking trail in the Pacific Northwest!

McLane Nature Trail

Getting there

Delphi Rd; Olympia, WA
Directions: From Olympia – Take the Evergreen State College exit from northbound Hwy 101. Take the Mud Bay Exit. Turn left at the stop sign and right again on Delphi Road. The trail is on your right.
Contact: (360)753.8380, olympiawa.gov

Visitor information

Hours: Daily to dusk
Cost: Free
Parking: Free parking where you can find it

Amenities

- Paved walking trail

About McLane Nature Trail

A pleasant maintained and paved walking trail with lines of beautiful blossoming daffodils in the spring that are planted and maintained by the children of the nearby McLane Elementary School. Along the trail you will find benches, informational signs, ponds, marsh lands, forest areas. Perfect for strolling or your morning walking routine, it is abundant with wildlife and nature to enjoy.

Bird houses line the trail making this an exceptional walk to bird watch.

Recommended Planner

Perfect trail for walking rain or shine as the path is paved. I couldn't find a designated parking lot for this trail, but there are some places to park along Delphi Road and Evergreen Parkway.

Mission Creek Nature Park

Getting there

1700 San Francisco Ave NE, Olympia, WA
Directions: From I-5 south, take exit 105 and take ramp toward Port of Olympia. Keep straight onto East Bay Drive, then keep straight onto Plum St SE and straight onto East Bay Drive NE. Turn right onto San Francisco Ave NE.
Contact: (360)753.8380, olympiawa.gov

Visitor information

Hours: Daily to dusk
Cost: Free
Parking: No dedicated parking

Amenities

- 37 acres
- 5 pedestrian entrances
- 1 mile crushed rock and soft surface trail

About Mission Creek Nature Park

Mission Creek Nature Park offers 37 acres with one mile of nature trails through forest and wetlands off San Francisco Avenue NE. Four additional pedestrian entrances from Ethridge Avenue NE, Fir Street, Edison Street NE and Lybarger Street make this nature trail accessible for locals. No dedicated parking is offered at any of the entrances, but accessible for explorers arriving by foot, bike or bus.

Old Capitol Building

Getting there

600 South Washington; Olympia, WA
Directions: From North I-5, Take exit 105 to Port of Olympia. Take Plum Street exit B. Follow Plum Street to Legion Way and turn left. Turn left onto Washington. The main entrance is on the left across from Sylvester Park.
Contact: (360)725-6000, www.olywa.org

Visitor information

Parking: City parking along streets may be metered.

Amenities

- State and National Historic Site
- Part of the Olympia Downtown Historic District Walking Tour

About the Old Capitol Building:

The Old Capitol Building is listed on both State and National Registers of Historic Places. The building has had many changes since the first opening in 1892 as the original Thurston County Courthouse. In 1901 the building was purchased for $350,000 and used as the State Capitol. In 1906 the Old Capitol Building became the home for the office of the Superintendent of Public Instruction. Fire gutted the tower and fourth floor in 1939, which prompted the construction of new concrete floors, and later in 1949 an earthquake resulted in the loss of 10 out of 12 towers and other parts of the building. Another earthquake in 1965 caused additional damage to the building. In February of 1983, a 9 million dollar project was completed restoring walls, ceilings, elevators, and adding a new skylight and new copper roof.

Olympia Center

Getting there

222 Columbia St. NW; Olympia, WA
Directions: From I-5 North, take exit 105 (Port of Olympia), Turn left onto Plum St., Left on State Ave, right on Columbia.
-or-
From I-5 South, Take exit 105B (Port of Olympia), onto Plum Street, Left on State Ave, Right on Columbia.
Contact: (360)753.8380, www.olympiawa.gov

Visitor information

Hours: See web site or call
Cost: Facility rental fees may apply
Parking: City parking along streets may be metered

Amenities:

- Public facility
- Event rentals
- Programs
- Classes

About Olympia Center

The Olympia Center is open to the public and all members of the community. Near Budd Inlet and Percival Landing in downtown Olympia, the Olympia Center offers programs and facility space. Olympia Center offers kitchen rentals, large event room, stage, nine meeting rooms, free parking, sound systems, tables, chairs, audio visual equipment and more. Olympia Center is also home to the Olympia Parks, Arts & Recreation Department and Senior Services for South Sound. A variety of classes are offered here. Check their web site for full detail on services offered, rental fees, and rules.

Olympia Skate Court

Getting there

3100 Capitol Mall Drive SW; Olympia, WA
Directions: From I-5 South, Take the US-101 N
Exit 104 to Aberdeen/ Port Angeles. Take the
Black Lake Blvd exit to West Olympia. Turn right
at Black Lake Blvd SW. Turn left at Cooper Point
Rd SW. Turn left at Capitol Mall Dr SW.
Contact: (360)753.8380, olympiawa.gov

Visitor information

Hours: Daily to dusk
Cost: Free
Parking: Free parking at Yauger Park

Amenities:

- 11,500 square feet
- Concrete skate surface
- Rules and regulations
- Vertical elements
- Bowl
- Grinding rails and snake runs

About Olympia Skate Court

Olympia Skate Court is located at Yauger Park in
Olympia off Capitol Mall Drive. With its grand
opening April 1, 2000, the Olympia Skate Court
offers an 11,500 square foot concrete surface for
skaters in the community. The court offers 5 feet
(or less) verticals, bowl, grinding rails and snake
runs for skateboards and rollerblades. Rules and
regulations are posted at the court and helmets
and pads are encouraged.

Olympia Timberland Regional Library

Getting there

313 8th Ave. SE; Olympia, WA
Directions: From I-5 South, take exit 105 to State Capitol / City Center / Port of Olympia. Bear right and head toward Plum St. SE and bear right at Plum St SE. Turn left at 8th Ave SE.
Contact: (360)352.0595, ww.timberland.lib.wa.us

Visitor information

Hours: Daily to dusk
Cost: Free
Parking: Free parking in lot

Amenities:

- Books
- Videotapes
- DVDs

- CDs
- Audio cassettes
- Newspapers
- Magazines
- All age programs
- Computers
- Internet
- Public meeting rooms

About Olympia Timberland Regional Library

The Olympia Library was established in 1896 by the Women's Club of Olympia. The library contained reading material donated by community members. The city took over in 1909 and it contained some 900 items. In 1968, the library became a part of the Timberland library district.

Today the library offers many amenities to community members. The library has for loan: books, videotapes, DVDs, CDs, audio cassettes, newspapers, and magazines for all age levels.

The library also offers computers with internet, online reference, databases and software for children.

Recommended Planner

Check the library schedule for programs going on for the age group you are interested in. Summer offers reading programs for youth and winter offers many indoor adventures through reading.

Olympia Woodland Trail

Getting there

1600 Eastside Street SE, Olympia, WA
Directions: From I-5 South, take the ramp toward Port of Olympia. Keep straight onto East Bay Dr, keep straight onto Plum St SE. Turn right onto Pear St SE, turn right onto Union Ave SE, then turn right onto Eastside St SE.
Contact: (360)753.8380, olympiawa.gov

Visitor information

Hours: Daily to dusk
Cost: Free
Parking: Free parking at trailhead

Amenities

- 2.5 mile trail
- Picnic shelter
- Restroom

About Olympia Woodland Trail

Once a rail line, Olympia Woodland Trail is now a 2.5 mile paved trail that connects east and west Olympia. The land was acquired in 2003 and the first section of the trail opened to the public in August of 2007. The trail extends from Eastside Street and Wheeler Avenue to the Chehalis Western Trail. Over 12,000 native trees and shrubs have been planted along the trail. Additional trailheads are accessible off Fredrick Street, Boulevard Road and Dayton Avenue.

Park of the Seven Oars

Getting there

Corner of West Bay Drive and Harrison Avenue; Olympia, WA
Directions: Located at the top of the 4th Avenue Bridge on the corner of West Bay Drive and Harrison Avenue.
Contact: (360)753.8380, olympiawa.gov

Visitor information

Hours: Daily to dusk
Cost: Free
Parking: Free parking can be found along side streets nearby

Amenities:

- Public art
- Historical Information
- View

About Park of the Seven Oars

The original Park of the Seven Oars was constructed in 1993 by artists Tom Anderson, Karen Lohmann, Mark Osborne and Joe Tougas in collaboration with Robert W. Droll, Landscape Architect. The Project combines natural and human-made objects. The park was moved across the street from the original site in 1999 when the 4th Avenue Bridge and roundabout were built.

Public art includes seven steel oars and Northwest Native American cedar canoes. The inspiration for the design came from a photograph taken in the 1890s of seven women holding oars at Priest Point Park in Olympia.

Recommended Planner

On a stroll along the waterfront, take a walk across the 4th Avenue Bridge and up to Park of the Seven Oars. Take in the view of the bay, Olympia, and enjoy the artwork.

Percival Landing

Getting there

217 Thurston Avenue NW; Olympia, WA
Directions: From I-5 South, Take the Pacific Ave
SE exit 107. Turn right at Pacific Ave SE. Bear
left at State Ave NE. Turn right at Jefferson St.
NE. Turn left at Thurston Ave NE.
Contact: (360)753.8380, olympiawa.gov

Visitor information

Hours: Daily to dusk
Cost: Free
Parking: Free parking along city streets or lots

Amenities:

- 3.38 acres
- Picnic tables
- Restrooms
- Showers
- Playground
- Public art
- Overnight boat moorage
- .9 mile boardwalk

About Percival Landing

Percival Landing gets its name from an old commercial steamship wharf operated by the Percival family. The landing has been built in three phases. The first phase was completed in 1978, the second in 1985 and the final phase was completed in 1988. Giving access to the Olympia waterfront, the boardwalk extends from the port of Olympia to the 4th Avenue Bridge.

Along your stroll on the boardwalk you will find historical kiosks and public art. A whale carved by Olympia artist Joe Tougas in 1981 was also duplicated for Olympia's sister city Yashiro, Japan. Another popular art feature is "The Kiss" which is a life size cast aluminum statue designed by Richard S. Beyer and dedicated July 6, 1990.

Another popular feature along the boardwalk is the Viewing Tower at the north end of the boardwalk near the Port Plaza and Farmers Market. Climb to the top for a spectacular view!

Recommended Planner

It is always a favorite to visit the Farmers Market or local restaurant and then take a stroll along the boardwalk. If you're heading toward the 4th Avenue Bridge, close by are Capital Lake and the Park of the Seven Oars.

Priest Point Park

Getting there

2600 East Bay Drive NE; Olympia, WA
Directions: From downtown, turn north on Plum Street which turns into East Bay Drive the park entrance is on the right.
Contact: (360)753.8380, olympiawa.gov

Visitor information

Hours: Daily to dusk
Cost: Free
Parking: Free parking in park

Amenities:

- Picnic shelters
- Restrooms
- Playground
- Basketball
- Nature trails
- Rose garden
- Memorial garden
- Benches
- Views
- Informative signs

About Priest Point Park

Established in 1848 by a group of French Catholic missionaries, the park is originally home of ancient Squaxin Island family villages. Later the park became the mission of the Oblates of Mary Immaculate. Priest Point Park became property of the city in 1905 and is the largest urban forest in the city boasting 1,000 feet of saltwater shoreline.

Today, Priest Point Park has towering trees, lush forest, shade, shelters, bridge and areas to explore. A garden offers flowering trees in spring and roses in summer. The park also offers a view point overlooking the sound, open grass areas to enjoy running, picnicking, family gatherings, or midday breaks from the bustle of life. Glider chairs are fun for sitting deep in thought or sharing a laugh with a young child.

Recommended Planner

Make a day of it! Bring friends, family or come alone. The playground makes a fantastic adventure for the little ones, while wide open spaces nearby provide plenty of room to play a game of Frisbee or ball.

Stevens Field

Getting there

300 24th Avenue SE; Olympia, WA
Directions: From I-5 South, take the State
Capitol / City Center / Port of Olympia Exit #105.
Follow 14th Avenue SE and turn left onto Capitol
Way S turn right on 24th Ave SW.
Contact: (360)753.8380, olympiawa.gov

Visitor information

Hours: Daily to dusk
Cost: Free
Parking: Free parking near fields

Amenities:

- 13 acres
- Picnic areas
- Basketball
- Tennis
- Athletic fields

About Stevens Field

On May 27, 1921 Stevens Field was deeded to the Olympia School District. The site was leased to the City of Olympia in 1963 for athletic use.

Adjacent to Lincoln Elementary School, the park remains a dynamic area for competitive games.

Recommended Planner

If you are looking for a sports field this is a quaint park and you are sure to find it here! Call the Olympia Parks and Recreation for more booking information. Pet stations are available for those who want to bring four-legged friends.

Sunrise Park

Getting there

500 Birch St. NW or 505 Bing St. NW; Olympia, WA

Directions: From US-101, take the Black Lake Blvd exit toward West Olympia. Merge onto Black Lake Blvd SW and it will become Division St. NW. Turn left onto Jackson Avenue NW. Turn right onto Bing St. NW.

Contact: (360)753.8380, olympiawa.gov

Visitor information

Hours: Daily to dusk
Cost: Free
Parking: Free parking in lot on Bing Street

Amenities

- 5.74 acres
- Picnic areas
- Playground
- Basketball
- Playfield
- Walking trail

About Sunrise Park

Opened and dedicated in 1995, Sunrise Park was a joint effort between the Westside Neighborhood Association and The Olympia Parks, Arts & Recreation Department.

A winding trail to the top of the park is said to offer views of Mt. Rainier and beautiful sunrise. A paved trail offers young bikers a great ride, playground offers plenty of fun, and the wide open grassy space offers ample of outdoor adventure.

Recommended Planner

A basketball area features hoops and hopscotch area. Bring your own ball for a game and no matter your age, take a hop and skip on the hopscotch! For the little ones, bring some sand toys – there is a great sand box at the playground. There is no shade at this park, so remember the sun block.

Swantown Marina

Getting there

1022 Marine Drive NE; Olympia, WA
Directions: Take Exit 105B. Stay right and follow the Port of Olympia signs onto Plum Street.   Go through six (6) traffic lights. The last light will be State Avenue. After crossing State Avenue, turn left onto Marine Drive, just past the Shell Gas Station. Marine Drive "forks" right; Swantown Boatworks will be on your right just before the "fork." Stay to the right and continue on Marine Drive to the Swantown Marina.
Contact: (360)528-8000, www.portolympia.com

Visitor information

Hours: Hours vary by season
Cost: See web site for Marina Rates. Paths are free for walking / strolling.
Parking: $3 parking per night or find free parking on nearby streets.

Amenities

- Gravel walking path
- Views

About Swantown Marina

Located between the Farmers Market and the Eastbay Waterfront Park, Swantown has moorage for your boat, or simply enjoy the beauty of Olympia. Take a stroll on the gravel-walking path or boat watch – Swantown can be added to your places to visit in a walking tour of Olympia.

Swantown, owned by the Port of Olympia, has been providing Puget Sound day-use access and boat moorage since 1983. Many additional amenities are offered for moorage guests – such as shore facilities, a future marina village and more.

Sylvester Park

Getting there

Capitol Way and Legion Way; Olympia, WA
Directions: Head Northwest on Plum Street SE,
Turn left on Legion Way. The park is between
Legion Way, Capitol Way, Washington St SE and
Seventh Ave SE in downtown Olympia.

Visitor information

Hours: Daily to dusk
Cost: Free
Parking: Metered or free parking along Olympia
streets

Amenities:

- Gazebo
- Statues
- Art
- Benches

About Sylvester Park

Listed on both the National and Washington State Registers of Historic Places, Sylvester Park is the heart and soul of Olympia. Olympia's founder Edmund Sylvester platted his town in 1850. Sylvester put one downtown block aside for an open public square. Settlers built a blockhouse here in 1855 to fit an entire village population inside during the Puget Sound Indian War. Once threats of war passed, the blockhouse became Olympia's city jail.

In 1893, the old town square was officially named Sylvester Park and beautifully landscaped about the time the Old Capitol Building across the street opened as the Thurston County Courthouse. Landscaping included beech and maple trees, paths made of crushed clamshells, a pond, and a Victorian Bandstand.

During World War I, the original bandstand was vandalized and then torn down in 1928. A new bandstand was constructed in 1976.

During the summer months, free concerts can be found here at Sylvester Park. In the winter months, the trees are covered in holiday lights.

Trillium Park

Getting there

900 Governor Stevens Ave SE -or- 901 Eskridge
Blvd. SE; Olympia, WA
Directions: From Governor Stevens Ave follow
to Hoadly Road.
Contact: (360)753.8380, olympiawa.gov

Visitor information

Hours: Daily to dusk
Cost: Free
Parking: Free parking along neighborhood
streets

Amenities

- 4.53 acres
- Nature trail
- Bench
- Forested
- Steps

About Trillium Park

Donated by property owners in the late 1980s, this scenic ravine offers a trail from Hoadly Street linking Governor Stevens Neighborhood to the Wildwood Neighborhood.

Recommended Planner

A nice little walk through beautiful neighborhoods and into beautiful forest makes this an enjoyable little adventure.

Washington State Capitol Campus

Getting there

416 14th Avenue; Olympia, WA
Directions: From I-5 take Exit 105 State Capitol / City Center / Port of Olympia. Follow signs to State Capitol. Located on 14th Ave SE.
Contact: (360)586.8687, olympiawa.gov

Visitor information

Hours: September - May
Monday – Friday 8am-5pm
Summer: Monday – Friday 8am-5pm
Saturday & Sunday 10-4

Cost: Free
Parking: Capitol Visitor Lot at Jefferson Street and Wheeler Avenue.
Visitor Information Center at 14th and Capitol Way.
General Administration Parking Garage at 11th Avenue and Columbia Street.

Parking is 50 cents per hour payable at meters in each parking area.

Free parking available on the east side of Capitol Way.

Amenities:

- Public guided hourly or specialty tours
- Executive mansion tours
- Self guided tours
- Snack and espresso bar
- Cafeteria
- Conservatory
- Memorials and monuments

About Washington State Capitol Campus

Completed in 1928, The State Capitol Campus and Legislative Building were the last greatest domed capitol to be built in America. This domed beauty designed in a mixture of Roman, Green and neo Classical style stands 28 stories high upon a bluff overlooking the Puget Sound. The 42 expansive granite steps leading up to the entrance represent Washington being the 42nd state in the Union.

The building was labored for five years by thirty artisans who carved the building's details from sandstone, marble and wood. At the base of the dome, stone ox skulls circle the base in a frieze that honors Washington's ox-cart pioneers. Inside you can find beautiful workmanship from the elaborate plaster ceilings down to the doorknobs bearing the official state seal.

The Visitor Information Center offers guided tours every hour on the hour between 10:00 am and 3:00 pm on operational days. Brochures and self-guided tour material are available for individuals who wish to tour without the group.

On the outside, the Capitol Campus offers over 30 acres of beautifully landscaped grounds with seasonal gardens, memorials, monuments, statues, and fountain. There is a conservatory which was constructed in 1939 by the Works Progress Administration. Inside the conservatory you will find cacti, orchids, and sub-tropical plants. It produces bedding plants for the Capitol Campus and is open to the public 8:00am – 3:00 pm weekdays. During the summer the hours may be extended so call for information.

On the inside, you will find the grand beauty and rich history of the Olympia Capitol. You can also find the Temple of Justice which was completed in 1912 and is home to the Washington State Supreme Court and the State Law Library. This is open to the public 8:00-5:00 pm Monday - Friday.

Tours of the Executive Mansion are available most Wednesdays by reservation only. To find out more information on this particular tour or other specialty tours, please contact the tour office at (360) 902.8880.

Recommended Planner

It is my recommendation that you take some time to visit the State Capitol Campus for a guided tour. Rich with history and beauty, it really is a must whether you are a native or new to the area. Be sure to wander the grounds after your tour. Sit in a garden or under a shaded tree, view the memorials and reflect. Be sure to bring your camera and some change for the parking meter.

Washington State Capitol Museum

Getting there

211 W. 21st Avenue; Olympia, WA
Directions: From I-5: Take Exit 105, Follow the State Capitol / City Center signs. Turn left on Capitol Way. Turn right on 21st Avenue. The museum is 2 blocks on the left.
Contact: (360)753.2580, olympiawa.gov

Visitor information

Hours:
Tuesday–Friday: 10am-4pm
Saturday: 12noon- 4pm
Sunday: Closed
Monday: Closed
Cost: Free to WSHS members and children less than 6yrs of age.
6yr-18yr: $1.00   18yr+: $2.00
60yr+: $1.75   Family: $5.00
Parking: Free parking curb side

Amenities:

- Historic museum
- Exhibits
- Native American History
- Temporary exhibits
- Ethno botanical garden
- Museum store

About Washington State Capitol Museum

This beautiful stucco mansion on 21st Avenue in Olympia is six blocks from the Washington State Capitol Campus and rich with history. The exhibits here are a tribute to the history and culture of Washington State. Here you can learn about regional Native American History, the construction of the Capitol building, and many other informative exhibits.

Outside the museum, stroll through the beautiful ethno botanical gardens full of northwest plant life.

The Museum also offers group tours or school field trips by reservation.

Recommended Planner

This is a fantastic spot to bring out of town guests or anyone interested in the history of the area. If you have lived here and have yet to go yourself, take some time and visit yourself.

Watershed Park

Getting there

2820 Henderson Blvd SE; Olympia, WA
(Pedestrian)
1605 Eastside St. SE; Olympia, WA (Pedestrian)
1201 22nd Ave. SE; Olympia, WA (Pedestrian)
2500 Henderson Blvd SE; Olympia, WA (Parking)
Directions: To the parking area: From I-5, take
the State Capitol/ City Center/ Port of Olympia
exit # 105. Follow East Bay Drive and turn left at
Henderson Blvd SE.
Contact: (360)753.8380, olympiawa.gov

Visitor information

Hours: Daily to dusk
Cost: Free
Parking: Free parking in a small lot off
Henderson Blvd SE

Amenities

- 153 acres
- 1.5 mile loop nature trail

About Watershed Park

During the late 1800s and early 1900s, the city
used this site known historically as Moxlie Creek
and surrounding artisan wells as a water source.
In 1955 the area was to be sold and logged, but
after the community protested, the area was
protected.

In 1977 a work experience class through Olympia High School built a 1.5 mile walking trail through Olympia's old watershed and named it G. Eldon Marshall Trail after Olympia's long time city manager.

Today this beautiful 153-acre park has a 1.5 mile maintained nature trail through temperate rain forest dripping with moss, boardwalks over swamplands, 28 springs, and glimpses of Mox Moxie Creek.

Recommended Planner

Wear sturdy shoes, come prepared with water, and bug spray. Steep inclines have stairs to be aware of. Four-legged friends are welcome as long as they are on a leash.

West Bay Park

Getting there

700 West Bay Drive NW
Directions: From downtown Olympia, follow 4th
Ave West, at the roundabout, take the first exit
onto Olympic Way NW. At the roundabout, take
the first exit onto West Bay Dr NW. The
destination is on your right along the water.
Contact: (360)753.8380, olympiawa.gov

Visitor information

Hours: Daily to dusk
Cost: Free
Parking: Free parking

Amenities

- 17 acres (4 acres developed)
- Benches
- Views
- Walking paths

About West Bay Park

Opened on July 14, 2010, West Bay Park offers
views of the State Capitol, water views and views
of the Olympic Mountains.

Recommended planner

Come enjoy the views or bring your Kayak to
explore the shoreline.

William Cannon Foot Path

Getting there

Madrona Beach Road; Olympia, WA
Directions: From Olympia, take the 2nd Avenue and Mud Bay Exit off US 101, and turn right onto Mud Bay Road. Turn left onto Madrona Beach Road. Park in the Park and Ride Lot on the right.
Contact: (360)866.9124

Visitor information

Hours: Daily to dusk
Cost: Free
Parking: Free parking in the WA DOT Park and Ride

Amenities:

- Nature trail
- Views
- Informative signs
- Historical marker

About William Cannon Footpath

This trail is located off the back side of the Washington State Department of Transportation Park and Ride off Madrona Beach Road. It is named for William Cannon who came to the Pacific Northwest in 1810 with the Astor expedition and created the first flour mill on the Pacific Coast.

The coordination of this footpath was an effort by the McLane School Forest and Trail Committee and offers interpretive markers, a gravel footpath and beautiful views of Eld Inlet (also known in the area as Mud Bay). At the head of the trail you will find 3 signs describing the history of the area. As you continue down the trail past chain link fencing, you will find small paths leading off the main path to the water.

Recommended planner

While the trailhead does not look like much, be sure to wander far enough to see the water. The views are especially nice when the tide is in. At one point a small path went off the trail and we found an orange bench that offered a nice reflective stop in our adventure. In the summer enjoy the sweet smells of blackberries that grow all along the trail.

Woodard Bay Conservation Area

Getting there

Woodard Bay Road; Olympia, WA
Directions: From Olympia go North on Plum Street which becomes East Bay Drive, then Boston Harbor Road. Turn right on Woodard Bay. Turn left on Libby then an immediate right back onto Woodard Bay. There is a small parking area at the base of the hill, and a large lot ¼ mile further on the left.
Contact: (360)577.2025, www.dnr.wa.gov

Visitor information

Hours: Daily to dusk
Cost: Free
Parking: Free parking in both lots

Amenities:

- 600 acres
- 2 nature trails
- Informative signs
- Toilet
- Benches

About Woodard Bay Conservation Area

Originally home to American Indian settlement in the 1850s and later Puget Sound's logging area; Woodard Bay Conservation Area is the perfect spot to learn about the early uses of this site.

Woodard Bay Conservation Area was established in 1987 by the Washington Department of Natural Resources. This conservation covers 600 acres of forest and wet land and offers two trails: a forested loop and a barrier free view of Woodard Bay. It is said to be an excellent place to bird watch, as 175 species of birds have been recorded – from bald eagles, great blue herron, to a colony of bats and more. You might also spot river otters, mink and harbor seals along the shore.

Note that in effort to protect nesting bald eagles the forested loop trail is closed during nesting season and no pets are allowed.

Recommended Planner

Bring a sense of adventure, a good pair of binoculars and a camera. The views are especially nice when the tide is in.

Woodruff Park

Getting there

1500 Harrison Ave; Olympia, WA
Directions: From US-101, take the Black Lake
Blvd exit to West Olympia. Turn right at Black
lake Blvd. Continue on Division St. NW. Turn
right at Harrison Ave NW.
Contact: (360)753.8380, olympiawa.gov

Visitor information

Hours: Daily to dusk
Cost: Free
Parking: Free parking along street

Amenities

- 2.38 acres
- Picnic areas
- Restrooms
- Basketball
- Tennis
- Sand volleyball

About Woodruff Park

Woodruff Park is Olympia's first park. The park is named after Sam Woodruff who was a printer and bookseller and one of Olympia's first land developers. In 1892, Woodruff sold the land to the city for $1 to be used as a park.

On Olympia's west side, this park is located off a busy road near Garfield Elementary School. Today it offers sports activities, open grass areas, big trees and flowering bulbs.

Recommended Planner

This is a nice park for some athletic adventure. Bring your tennis gear and a friend!

Yashiro Japanese Garden

Getting there

1010 Plum Street SE; Olympia, WA
Directions: Head north on Capitol Way South
toward 11th Ave SW. Turn right onto Union Ave
SE. Turn left onto Plum St SE. The garden will
be on your right.
Contact: (360)753.8380, olympiawa.gov

Visitor information

Hours: Daily to dusk
Cost: Free
Parking: Free parking in the lot

Amenities:

- .74 acres
- Paths
- Pond
- Waterfall
- Benches

About Yashiro Japanese Garden

Honoring Olympia's sister city Yashiro, Japan, this traditional Asian garden was dedicated in May of 1990. Designed by Robert Murase and built with the help of 75 volunteers you will find a classic gate, cut stone lanterns, 13-tier pagoda, a pond with waterfall, and winding paths through rhododendrons, flowering trees, and flowers.

Pets are welcome as long as they are on a leash and pet waste is properly disposed of.

Recommended Planner

This is a surprising place to come in the city where you can sit, reflect, and enjoy the peaceful tranquility around you. While here I saw one man strumming on a guitar playing a soft song.

Yauger Park

Getting there

3100 Capital Mall Drive SW; Olympia, WA
-or- 530 Alta Street SW
Directions: From Hwy 101, take Black Lake Blvd
exit and head north on Black Lake Blvd. Turn left
on Cooper Point Road. Turn left on Capitol Mall
Drive. Turn right behind Apple Park Apartments
(Alta Street), the park is straight ahead.
Contact: (360)753.8380, olympiawa.gov

Visitor information

Hours: Daily to dusk
Cost: Free
Parking: Free parking off Alta Street SW

Amenities

- 39.77 acres
- Picnic shelter
- Restrooms
- Playground
- Sports fields
- Seasonal concession stand
- Horseshoe
- Skate court
- Nature trail
- Jogging path

About Yauger Park

Developed in 1982, Yauger Park serves as a community park and a storm water detention area. It is named for United States Army Colonel Yauger who had a vision for this multi-purpose site.

The park's fields are popular in the summer months for baseball games and soccer in the fall. The fields fill with water in the winter and activities pause until the fields dry again in the summer.

An unexpected nature trail developed by Capitol High School students can be found near the parking lot which offers winding trails, board walks, and informative signs. There is also a composting and demonstration garden near the trail head. Information about the demonstration garden can be found by calling the Master Gardeners Foundation at (360)786.5445.

A skate park can be found near the northwest corner. For information about the skate park see Olympia Skate Court.

In more recent years, the park has undergone many improvements including a bridge and community garden.

Recommended Planner

This is a fun park for every age. From playing baseball in the summer, to strolling through the nature trail, to playing on the large playground, to walking your pet, everyone is sure to find something of interest here. If you have been here but it has been a while, come check out what is new!

Part 2 - Tumwater, WA

South of Olympia and located at the mouth of the Deschutes River, Tumwater is one of the oldest permanent American settlements on Puget Sound. Founded in 1845 by Michael T. Simmons and his group, it was first named New Market and in 1963 became known as Tumwater which means waterfall in Chinook. Tumwater offers views of the Olympic Mountains and Mount Rainier. Today, Tumwater is the third largest city in Thurston County covering over 11 square miles.

5th and Grant Pocket Park

Getting there

5th and Grant Streets; Tumwater, WA
Directions: From Olympia, head south on I-5 toward Portland. Take the 2nd Avenue Exit #103. Turn right onto Desoto St. SW. (First right off the freeway). Desoto turns into 4th Ave SW. Turn left on Ferry St. SW. Turn right onto N 5th Ave SW. The park is on the corner of 5th Avenue and Grant. There is a road closed sign at the end of 5th Avenue – the park is to the left of this sign.
Contact: (360)754.4160, www.ci.tumwater.wa.us

Visitor information

Hours: Daily to dusk
Cost: Free
Parking: Free parking

Amenities

- .3 acres
- Small play toy
- Basketball hoop
- Scenic overlook
- Trees / Shade

About 5th and Grant Pocket Park

Located at 5th and Grant Streets, this pocket park offers a small play toy, basketball hoop and a scenic overlook. Tucked in a corner, it is a small treasure when you find it.

Capitol Little League Field

Getting there

7700 New Market Street SW; Tumwater, WA
Directions: From I-5 South, Take exit 101 for Tumwater Blvd toward Olympia Airport. Turn left at Tumwater Blvd SW. At the traffic circle, take the first exit onto New Market Street SW.
Contact: www.capitollittleleague.com

Visitor information

Hours: For field use, contact Capitol Little
League
Cost: Free
Parking: Free parking along the road

Amenities

- Baseball Fields
- Playground

About Capitol Little League Fields:

Seven baseball fields next to the Olympia Airport
off New Market Street, home to Capitol Little
League. New Market Street Playground is part of
this play park.

Henderson House Museum

Getting there

602 Deschutes Way; Tumwater, WA
Directions: From Olympia, Take Capitol Way S.
and turn right onto E S. SW. Take a slight right
onto Deschutes Way.
Contact: (360)754.4217, www.ci.tumwater.wa.us

Visitor information

Hours: Thursday, Friday, Sunday 1pm – 4pm
Cost: Suggested Donation: $2 for adults
$1 for children ages 12-18
Free for children under 12
Parking: Free parking

Amenities

- Historic House
- Museum
- Pioneer Log Cabin

About Henderson House Museum

Built in 1905 by the Olympia Manufacturing and Building Company, the Henderson House was first home to William Naumann who was a Brewmaster for the Olympia Brewery. Built in a traditional Queen Anne design, the home underwent several owners before being purchased in 1939 by James F. and Agnes Henderson.

To learn more about this historic home, and to view hundreds of photographs of early Tumwater, the Olympia Brewery and more, stop by the museum. It is open Thursdays, Fridays and Sundays from 1 to 4pm.

A Pioneer Log Cabin built in 1969 by Weldon Rau of Olympia in memory of his pioneer grandparents who crossed the Oregon Trail. Donated in the early 1980s to the City of Tumwater.

Historic Crosby House Museum

Getting there

702 Deschutes Way N. Tumwater, WA
Directions: From Olympia, Take Capitol Way S. and turn right onto E S. SW. Take a slight right onto Deschutes Way.
Contact: (360)943.9884, www.ci.tumwater.wa.us

Visitor information

Hours: Mid March – mid-November:
Thursday & Sunday 1pm to 4pm
Summer Hours:
Thursday, Friday & Sunday 1pm to 4pm
Cost: Donations are suggested
Parking: Free parking at the house

Amenities

- Historic house
- Museum

About Historic Crosby House Museum

Built in 1860 by Nathaniel Crosby III, the Crosby House was home to him and his wife Cordelia Jane Smith until 1872. Between 1872 and 1941, the house was home to other local families – the Ostranders, the Hahns, the Cuylers, and the Parkers. In 1941 the house was purchased and donated to the Daughters of the Pioneers of Washington. In 1978 the house was given to the city of Tumwater. The Home has been restored and furnished since and offers a garden with historic cherry tree.

Recommended Planner

To learn more about the history of this house, be sure to stop in for a tour. The hours are limited so check the times to the season. Ask about the shadow box wreath!

Historical Park

Getting there

777 Simmons Rd. SW; Tumwater, WA
Directions: From Olympia, Take Capitol Way S. and turn right onto E S. SW. Take a slight right onto Deschutes Way. Turn past the Crosby House onto Simmons.
Contact: (360)754.4160, www.ci.tumwater.wa.us

Visitor information

Hours: Daily to dusk
Cost: Free
Parking: Free parking in a large lot

Amenities

- 17 acres
- Shelter
- Picnic facilities
- Restrooms
- Large and small play structures
- River access
- Trails
- Horse shoes
- Wide open grass areas
- Dog station

About Historical Park

This beautiful park was built in 1980 and covers 17 acres at the base of the falls and near the Crosby House. The park offers plenty of open space, picnicking opportunity and nature trails.

Recommended Planner

Historical Park is an excellent place for adventure. Bring a blanket for a picnic or your horseshoes for a game with friends.

Jim Brown Park

Getting there

5th and Bates; Tumwater, WA
Directions: From I-5, exit in Tumwater at 2nd
Ave. Continue on N. 2nd Ave SW and turn right
at Division St. SW. Turn right at N. 5th Avenue
SW.
Contact: (360)754.4160, www.ci.tumwater.wa.us

Visitor information

Hours: Daily to dusk.
Cost: Free
Parking: Free parking

Amenities

- Play toy
- ½ basketball court
- Tennis court
- Picnic area

About Jim Brown Park

Located near 5th and Bates Streets, Jim Brown park is a newer park on Tumwater Hill. Once Tumwater's Public Works Shop site, the park in now completed form offers a playground, basketball, tennis, and picnic opportunities.

KOMPAN

Getting there

7717 New Market; Tumwater, WA
Directions: From I-5, take the Tumwater Blvd SW exit 101 to Olympia Airport. Turn left at Tumwater Blvd SW. Turn right at New Market St. SW.
Contact: (360)754.4160, www.ci.tumwater.wa.us

Visitor information

Hours: Daily to dusk
Cost: Free
Parking: Free parking along New Market

Amenities:

- Playground

About KOMPAN

Located in Tumwater near the airport, KOMPAN manufactures playground systems and equipment. A sampling of their playground systems can be found on this location. Designed for children 5-12 years of age, it offers a bark base, climbing surfaces, suspended chairs to recline, rock climbing, and plenty of twisting, spinning and twirling fun for everyone.

Recommended Planner

The sole purpose here is TO PLAY! Adults and children alike will love playing here. Come find your inner child and make yourself dizzy as you spin out of control.

New Market Street Playground

Getting there

New Market Street; Tumwater, WA
Contact: See Capitol Little League Fields.

Overlook Point Park

Getting there

1205 Barnes Blvd; Tumwater, WA
Directions: From US 101, Take the Cooper Point Rd exit to Crosby Blvd / Automall Dr SW. Turn left at Cooper Point Rd. SW and continue on Crosby Blvd SW. Turn left at Barnes Blvd.
Contact: (360)754.4160, www.ci.tumwater.wa.us

Visitor information

Hours: Daily to dusk
Cost: Free
Parking: Free parking

Amenities:

- Scenic overlook
- Parking
- Picnic facilities
- Pet Station

About Overlook Point Park

Overlook Point Park offers breathtaking views of Mount Rainer on a clear day, and daily picnicking. The neighborhoods surrounding Overlook Point Park are increasing in numbers.

Recommended Planner

This is a great place to enjoy the views of the Capitol Building and Mount Rainer.

View from Overlook Point Park.

Palermo Pocket Park

Getting there

Palermo and O Street; Tumwater, WA
Directions: Call Tumwater Parks and Recreation for directions.
Contact: (360)754.4160, www.ci.tumwater.wa.us

Visitor information

Hours: Daily to dusk
Cost: Free
Parking: Free parking

Amenities:

- .3 acres
- Play toy
- Basketball hoop
- .7 mile looped nature / running path

About Palermo Pocket Park

Adjacent to the Tumwater Valley Golf Course, Palermo Pocket Park has a playground, basketball hoop and looped path.

Pioneer Park

Getting there

5900 Henderson Blvd SE; Tumwater, WA
Directions: From I-5, take the 2nd Avenue exit
#103 to Tumwater. Continue on N 2nd Ave SW.
Turn left at Custer Way SW. Turn right at
Cleveland Ave. SE. Bear left at Yelm Hwy SE.
Turn right at Henderson Blvd SE.
Contact: (360)754.4160, www.ci.tumwater.wa.us

Visitor information

Hours: Daily to dusk
Cost: Free
Parking: Free parking

Amenities:

- 85 acres
- Baseball field
- 2 softball fields
- 3 soccer fields
- 2 sand volleyball courts
- Children's play toys
- Restrooms
- Trails
- Deschutes River access
- Pet station
- Pay phone

About Pioneer Park

Land for this park was purchased in 1987 by the city of Tumwater. Completed in phases, this park is continually expanding to add more features. Pioneer Park is Tumwater's largest park covering 85 acres. It offers athletic fields, playgrounds, restrooms, and access to the Deschutes River. A ½ mile nature trail loops through open meadows and riverside woods with paved and unpaved surfaces.

Somerset Hill & SPSCC Trail

Getting there

Mottman Road; Tumwater
Directions: From I-5, take exit 104 HWY 101 exit toward the Ocean Beaches. Take the first exit on 101. Turn left onto Crosby Blvd. Cross over HWY 101 and turn right onto Mottman Road. The college is on the left. Enter from Lot A on campus.
Contact: (360)754.4160, www.ci.tumwater.wa.us

Visitor information

Hours: Daily to dusk
Cost: Free
Parking: $2 all day parking passes available at the South Puget Sound Community College parking lot off Mottman Road.

Amenities

- Walking trail – Not maintained
- Restrooms on campus
- Salmon viewing
- Bridge built by Boy Scouts

About Somerset Hill & SPSCC Trail

The Somerset Hill and SPSCC (South Puget Sound Community College) trails intersect at the east edge of the college campus. The .5 mile SPSCC trail follows Percival Creek, and the Somerset Hill pathway is .75 miles that parallels Somerset Hill Drive. These trails are not maintained. Use at your own risk.

Tumwater Falls Park

Getting there

C Street and Deschutes Way; Tumwater, WA
Directions: From I-5, take the 2nd Ave Exit #103. Continue on N 2nd Ave SW. Turn left at Custer Way SW. Turn right at Boston St. SE. Turn left at Deschutes Way SW.
Contact: (360)943.2550

Visitor information

Hours: Daily to dusk
Cost: Free
Parking: Free parking

Amenities

- Open grass
- Playground
- Restrooms
- Soda machine

- Drinking fountain
- Informational signs
- Walking trail
- Fish ladder
- Waterfall
- Picnic tables

About Tumwater Falls Park

Opened in 1962, Tumwater Falls Park is one of the last privately owned parks in Washington State. Site was first settled upon by some 30 pioneers where water powered sawmill and gristmill was built. A historic brick house built in 1906 belonging to Leopold Schmidt can be seen from the park.

15 acres of park boast open grass areas, playground, walking trails and views of the waterfall. Salmon fish ladders were built along the river's edge. Chinook and Coho salmon travel upstream in October and early November.

Tumwater Hill Park

Getting there

3115 Ridgeview Ct. SW; Tumwater, WA
Directions: From I-5 S, take the US-101 N. Exit
#104 to Aberdeen/ Port Angeles. Take Cooper
Point Road exit to Crosby Blvd/ Automall Dr.
SW. Turn left at Cooper Point Road SW.
Continue on Crosby Blvd. SW. Turn left at
Barnes Blvd SW. Turn right at Ridgeview Ct.
SW. Next to Tumwater Hill Elementary.
Contact: (360)754.4160, www.ci.tumwater.wa.us

Visitor information

Hours: Daily to dusk
Cost: Free
Parking: Free parking

Amenities

- 9 acres
- Youth baseball field
- Picnic areas
- ¾ mile trail

About Tumwater Hill Park

Offering a .5 mile looped nature trail with surface of bark and hard packed dirt. The trail head is located at Ridgeview Ct. SW.

V Street Pocket Park

Getting there

415 V Street SW; Tumwater, WA
Directions: From I-5 South, take the Trosper Rd. SW exit 102 to Black Lake. Turn right at Capitol Blvd SW. Turn right at W X St. SE. Turn right at 3rd Ave SW. Turn right at W St SW. Bear left at Janet Dr. SW, bear left at V St. SW.
Contact: (360)754.4160, www.ci.tumwater.wa.us

Visitor information

Hours: Daily to dusk
Cost: Free
Parking: Free parking

Amenities:

- Play toy
- Basketball court

About V Street Pocket Park

The trees in Pocket Park offer shade within a fenced area. V Street Pocket Park offers a play toy and basketball court. This park backs an industrial area. There are no bathrooms at this park.

Part 3 - Lacey, WA

Officially incorporated in December of 1966, Lacey neighbors Olympia. Known for its lakes, forests and beautiful Nisqually Valley, Lacey is a quiet city full of adventure.

Avonlea Park

Getting there

112 Ingleside Loop SE, Lacey, WA
Directions: From I-5, take the College St exit and follow College St south to 45th. At the roundabout take the first exit onto 45th Ave SE. Turn right onto Avonlea Dr SE.
Contact: (360)491.0857, ci.lacey.wa.us

Visitor information

Hours: Daily to dusk
Cost: Free
Parking: Free parking along Ingleside Loop SE

Amenities

- 5.4 acres
- Picnic shelter
- Tables
- Barbeques
- Half court basketball
- Playground
- Open space

About Avonlea Park

Dedicated in 1993, Avonlea Park is a neighborhood park that offers 5.4 acres of exploration and adventure.

Recommended planner

Bring your lawn games; there is plenty of open space to enjoy with your friends and family.

Brooks Park

Getting there

1313 College St. SE; Lacey, WA
Directions: From I-5, take the Exit 107 for Pacific Avenue. Turn right on Pacific Avenue SE. Continue onto Lacey Blvd SE. Turn right at College St. SE
The park is west of College Street between 13th and 14th Avenue. (Look for the brown "Brooks Park Sign.")
Contact: (360)491.0857, www.ci.lacey.wa.us

Visitor information

Hours: Daily to dusk
Cost: Free
Parking: Free parking

Amenities:

- 1 acre
- Picnic facilities

About Brooks Park

A quiet 1-acre park, Brooks Park is located near the commercial core area of Lacey. It offers limited picnic facilities, grass and a great mix of shade and sun. There are no restroom facilities at this park.

Hawks Prairie Reclaimed Water Ponds

Getting there

Hogum Bay Road; Lacey, WA
Directions: From I-5, Take the Marvin Road exit west. Turn right at Hogum Bay Road. You will pass the dump on your right and continue along this road. The gravel parking lot is on your left.
Contact: (360)528.5700, www.lottonline.org

Visitor information

Hours: Daily to dusk
Cost: Free
Parking: Free parking

Amenities:

- Gravel trails
- Views of Mt. Rainier
- Reclaimed water

- Wildlife
- Plants
- Four interpretive kiosks

About Hawks Prairie Reclaimed Water Ponds:

A reclaimed water project by the LOTT Alliance, the Hawks Prairie Reclaimed Water Ponds offer gravel paths through a tranquil park like setting. Educational opportunities are provided throughout your visit with interpretive kiosks with tips on water stewardship, rain gardens, reclaiming water, and the importance of native plants and trees.

Homman Park (Al Anna Homman)

Getting there

1301 Carpenter Road; Lacey, WA
Directions: From I-5, take the Martin Way E. exit (#109) and turn right at Martin Way E. Turn right at Carpenter Rd SE. The park is off Alanna Drive.
Contact: (360)491.0857, www.ci.lacey.wa.us

Visitor information

Hours: Daily to dusk
Cost: Free
Parking: Free parking

Amenities:

- 8 acres
- Ball field
- Mini soccer field
- 3 multipurpose courts
- Running track
- Playground
- Restrooms
- Drinking water
- Pet station

About Homann Park

Homann Park in Lacey is a recreational park for athletic youth. A playground and restrooms make this an enjoyable outing for families.

Horizon Pointe Park

Getting there

5700 Balustrade Blvd SE, Lacey, WA
Directions: From I-5, take the College St exit
and follow College south. Turn left onto Lacey
Blvd SE, turn right onto Ruddell Rd SE and keep
straight as it turns into Yelm Hwy SE. Turn right
onto Balustrade Blvd SE.
Contact: (360)491.0857, ci.lacey.wa.us

Visitor information

Hours: Daily to dusk
Cost: Free
Parking: Free parking on the street

Amenities

- 9.5 acres
- Picnic shelter
- Barbeque
- Basketball court
- Soccer fields
- Open space
- Play structure

About Horizon Pointe Park

Dedicated to the City of Lacey in 1998, the
Horizon Pointe Park was developed in 2005 in
conjunction with the neighboring subdivision of
the same name.

Recommended planner

Enjoy the nice open space or shade from a
nearby tree followed by a picnic.

Jacob Smith House

Getting there

4500 Intelco Loop SE; Lacey, WA
Directions: From I-5, take exit #108 and follow signs to College Street. Turn right onto College Street. Turn right onto Corporate Center Drive and follow to Intelco Loop. Turn right on Intelco Loop. The first driveway on the right will lead you to the parking lot.
Contact: (360)491.0857, www.ci.lacey.wa.us

Visitor information

Hours: By reservation
Cost: Call for information
Parking: Free parking in the lot

Amenities

- Historic Home
- Events by Reservation

About Jacob Smith House

The oldest home in Lacey, the Jacob Smith House was built before the Civil War. The original property was 440 acres and was home to Jacob Smith, his wife Priscilla and their seven children. One might be surprised to learn that one of their great grand children was the famous Bing Crosby as their oldest daughter Cordelia Jane Smith had married Nathaniel Crosby III of Tumwater at the home in 1860.

Today the house serves as a place of social gatherings. On reservation, the house hosts weddings, reunions, meetings and retreats.

Lacey Community Center

Getting there

6729 Pacific Avenue SE; Lacey, WA
Directions: From I-5, take exit #107 to Pacific
Ave SE. Bear right onto Pacific Avenue SE and
continue onto Lacey Blvd. SE and then again
onto Pacific Avenue. The Community Center is
on your right.
Contact: (360)491.0857, www.ci.lacey.wa.us

Visitor information

Hours: Daily to dusk
Cost: Free
Parking: Free parking

Amenities

- 9,000 square foot multi-purpose facility
- Banquet and meeting rooms

About Lacey Community Center

Located at Woodland Creek Community Park, the Community Center offers large banquet room, meeting rooms, a kitchen and a lobby.

Lacey Timberland Library

Getting there

500 College St. SE; Lacey, WA
Directions: From I-5, Take the Sleater-Kinney
Road exit #108 to College Street. Continue on
3rd Ave SE and turn right at College St. SE.
Follow the signs to the library off 6th Avenue SE.
Contact: (360)491.0857, timberland.lib.wa.us

Visitor information

Hours: Monday – Thursday: 10am – 8pm
Friday & Saturday: 10am – 5pm
Sunday: 1pm – 5pm
Cost: Free
Parking: Free parking in lot

Amenities

- Books
- Videotapes
- DVDs
- CDs
- Audio cassettes
- Newspapers
- Magazines
- All age programs
- Computers
- Internet
- Public meeting rooms

About Lacey Timberland Library

Adjacent to the Lacey City Hall, this 20,000
square foot library opened in 1991.

Contact the library for information on classes and
events.

Lake Lois Park

Getting there

6020 7th Avenue SE; Lacey, WA
Directions: From I-5, take exit #109 to Martin
Way. Turn right onto Martin Way E. Turn right at
Carpenter Rd. SE. Turn right at 7th Ave SE.
Contact: (360)491.0857, www.ci.lacey.wa.us

Visitor information

Hours: Daily to dusk
Cost: Free
Parking: Free parking

Amenities

- 35.5 acres
- Pond
- Picnic table
- Drinking water
- Informational Signs
- Nature Trail

About Lake Lois Park

A small pond fed by Woodland Creek on 35.5 acres of Lake Lois Habitat Preserve and Interpretive Center. Explore wooded paths through trees, grass and natural vegetation. Watch for small wildlife and birds.

Lake Lois Reserve

Getting there

Carpenter Road; Lacey, WA
Directions: From I-5, take exit #109 to Martin Way. Turn right onto Martin Way E. Turn right at Carpenter Rd SE. The Reserve is across the street from Lake Lois Park.
Contact: (360)438.2671, www.ci.lacey.wa.us

Visitor information

Hours: Daily to dusk
Cost: Free
Parking: Free parking

Amenities

- 12 acre island
- Interpretive trail and signs

About Lake Lois Reserve

This reserve is a 12-acre island located near Lake Lois Park offering trails with informational signs. Douglas fir, Low Oregon grape, Beaked Hazelnut and other surprises wait at Lake Lois Reserve.

Lakepointe Park

Getting there

6400 Compton Blvd SE; Lacey, WA
Directions: From I-5 S, take the 2nd Ave exit to
Tumwater. Turn left at Custer Way SW. Turn
right at Cleveland Ave SE. Bear left at Yelm Hwy
SE and follow Yelm Hwy SE to Compton Blvd SE
where you will turn left.
Contact: (360)491.0857, www.ci.lacey.wa.us

Visitor information

Hours: Daily to dusk
Cost: Free
Parking: Free parking

Amenities

- 8 acres
- Picnic facilities
- Play fields
- Basketball
- Playground
- Tennis court
- Minimal shade
- Wetland ponds

About Lakepointe Park

A neighborhood park located off Compton Blvd, Lakepointe Park offers sports fields, basketball, tennis, as well as playground and picnic facilities. In June, redwing black birds were found to be dancing among the tall grasses in the ponds.

Long Lake Park

Getting there

2790 Carpenter Road; Lacey, WA
Directions: From I-5 N take the Martin Way E exit 109. Turn right onto Martin Way E. Turn right at Carpenter Rd SE.
Contact: (360)491.0857, www.ci.lacey.wa.us

Visitor information

Hours: Daily to dusk
Cost: Free

Parking: Free parking in the lot

Amenities

- 285 feet waterfront
- Swim area
- Picnic facilities
- Nature trail
- Sand Volleyball Court
- BBQs
- Bike rack
- Restrooms
- Lifeguard during posted times.
- Roped in swim area with dock

About Long Lake Park

Long Lake Park offers beautiful woods and walking trails as well as waterfront with swimming area. The park is near the Thurston County Fairgrounds. During sunny northwest days, the grass is covered with picnic blankets and the dock covered in sun bathing families.

Rainier Vista Community Park

Getting there

5475 45th Avenue SE; Lacey, WA
Directions: From I-5 take exit 107 to Pacific
Avenue. Turn right on Sleater Kinney Road SE.
Turn left at 14th Ave SE. Turn right at College St.
SE. Follow the round-about to 45th Ave SE.
Contact: (360)491.0857, www.ci.lacey.wa.us

Visitor information

Hours: Daily to dusk
Cost: Free
Parking: Free parking in the lot

Amenities

- 46 acres
- 3 soccer fields
- 3 baseball/softball fields
- Tennis court

- Sand volleyball
- Walkways
- Picnic facilities
- Restrooms
- Skate park

About Rainier Vista Community Park

This park offers plenty to do for the active adventurer. Athletic fields and courts, walkways, and a skate park are among the activities at Rainier Vista Community Park.

Regional Athletic Complex

Getting there

8345 Steilacoom Rd SE; Lacey, WA
Directions: From I-5 North, take the WA-510 exit 111 to Yelm. Turn right on Marvin Rd NE. Turn right at Steilacoom Rd SE.
Contact: (360)786.5595, www.co.thurston.wa.us

Visitor information

Hours: Daily to dusk
Cost: Free
Parking: Free parking

Amenities

- 4 soccer fields
- Restrooms
- Walking Trail
- 5 baseball fields
- Picnic facilities
- Playground

About Regional Athletic Complex

Also known as the RAC, this park currently offers 4 soccer fields, restrooms and a walking trail. There are plans to expand in the future to include baseball fields, picnicking facilities and a play ground.

If you are interested in scheduling a field, contact Thurston County Parks.

Thomas W. Huntamer Park

Getting there

618 Woodland Square Loop SE; Lacey, WA
Directions: From I-5, take exit 108 to Sleater-Kinney Rd. Turn right at Sleater Kinney Rd. SE. Turn left at 7th Ave SE. Turn right at Woodland Square Loop SE. The Park is within a business park.
Contact: (360)491.0857, www.ci.lacey.wa.us

Visitor information

Hours: Daily to dusk
Cost: Free
Parking: Free parking along the street

Amenities

- Picnic Facilities
- Event Stage
- Grass
- Shade
- Rock climbing
- Water fountain
- Restrooms

About Thomas W. Huntamer Park

Also known as Huntamer Park, this small park is offers picnic tables, benches, and an event stage. During the summer, Lacey Parks and Recreation hosts a free "In Tune" concert series. Also on stage find free summer movies in the park and the Lacey Idol competition.

Thornbury Park

Getting there

5500 Thornbury Drive SE; Lacey, WA
Directions: From I-5 South take the 2nd Ave SW exit toward Tumwater. Turn left at Custer Way SW. Turn right at Cleveland Ave SE. Bear left at Yelm Hwy SE and then turn left at Ruddell Rd SE. Turn right at 54th Ave SE. Turn right at Thornbury Dr. SE.
Contact: (360)491.0857, www.ci.lacey.wa.us

Visitor information

Hours: Daily to dusk
Cost: Free
Parking: Free parking

Amenities

- 9 acres
- Picnic shelter
- Playground
- Basketball hoop
- Pet station
- Water fountain
- BBQ
- Picnic tables

About Thornbury Park

A neighborhood park located on Thornbury Drive in Lacey, it offers a picnic shelter and a playground.

Wanschers Community Park

Getting there

2606 Hicks Lake Road SE; Lacey, WA
Directions: From I-5, take exit 107 to Pacific
Avenue SE. Follow through the round-about to
Lacey Blvd SE. Turn right at Ruddell Rd SE.
Turn left at 25th Ave SE. Turn right at Hicks Lake
Rd. SE.
Contact: (360)491.0857, www.ci.lacey.wa.us

Visitor information

Hours: Daily to dusk
Cost: Free
Parking: Free parking

Amenities

- 16 acres
- Lake
- Picnic Tables
- Paved and dirt paths

About Wanschers Community Park

This community park is located on Hicks Lake
and offers a calm wooded retreat. Future plans
include a swimming area.

William A. Bush Park

Getting there

4400 Chardonnay Dr. SE; Lacey, WA
Directions: From I-5 South, Take 2nd Ave ramp
to Tumwater. Continue on 2nd Avenue and turn
left on Custer Way SW. Turn right at Cleveland
Ave SE. Bear left at Yelm Hwy SE. Turn right at
Chardonnay Dr SE.
Contact: (360)491.0857, www.ci.lacey.wa.us

Visitor information

Hours: Daily to dusk
Cost: Free
Parking: Free parking along the curb

Amenities

- 8.5 acres
- Picnic shelter
- Playground

- Pet Station
- BBQs
- Park Benches

About William A. Bush Park

This park is 8.5 acres on Chardonnay Drive SE. It has a picnic shelter and a playground. Open grass and scattered large trees make shade as well as sun lovers happy.

Wonderwood Park

Getting there

5304 32nd Avenue SE; Lacey, WA
Directions: From I-5 North, take the Pacific Ave exit 107. Follow Pacific Ave SE until it turns into Lacey Blvd SE. Turn right at Ruddell Rd SE. Turn right at 32nd Ct. SE. (Access also from Brentwood Drive.)
Contact: (360)491.0857, www.ci.lacey.wa.us

Visitor information

Hours: Daily to dusk
Cost: Free
Parking: Free parking in the lot

Amenities

- 40 acres
- Paved trails
- Picnic shelter
- 2 softball / soccer fields
- 4 tennis courts
- Basketball court
- Playground

About Wonderwood Park

This large park in Lacey is part natural woodland that has a paved nature trail running through it and part recreational facility with athletic fields and courts. There is also a playground here.

Woodland Creek Community Park

Getting there

6729 Pacific Avenue SE; Lacey, WA
Directions: From I-5 North, take the Pacific Avenue exit 107. Pacific Avenue turns into Lacey Blvd SE and again turns into Pacific Avenue SE. The park is on your right.
Contact: (360)491.0857, www.ci.lacey.wa.us

Visitor information

Hours: Daily to dusk
Cost: Free
Parking: Free parking in the lot

Amenities

- 72 acres
- Pond
- Youth fishing
- Bathrooms
- Drinking fountain
- Bike rack
- Playground
- Picnic Shelter with BBQ stations
- Picnic Tables
- Paved trail

About Woodland Creek Community Park

Located at the Lacey Community Center, this 72-acre park is home to Long's Pond. The pond features fishing for ages 14 and under during daylight hours. The park also has ducks and geese. A new playground and picnic area make this a favorite treat for area families.

Part 4 - **Beyond Olympia**

Beyond Olympia, Tumwater and Lacey rest beautiful landscapes, amazing views, and some places to explore that deserve their place within these pages. While there are many more adventures to be had, here are a few that will begin your adventures outside Olympia, Tumwater and Lacey.

Millersylvania State Park

Getting there

12245 Tilley Rd S. Olympia, WA
Directions: Located 10 miles south of Olympia.
From I-5: Take exit #95. Drive east, and follow
signs to park (about three miles northeast of the
freeway.)
Contact: (360)748.2383, www.parks.wa.gov

Visitor information

Hours: Summer: 6:30am to 10pm
Winter: 8:00am to 5pm
Cost: The Discover Pass is required for motor-
vehicle access to state parks. Camping available
for a fee. (www.discoverpass.wa.gov)
Parking: See cost

Amenities:

- 842 acres
- Deep Lake access
- Camping
- Day use area
- Picnic facilities
- 8.6 mi. hiking trails
- Fishing
- Swimming
- Amphitheater
- Bird watching
- Horseshoes

About Millersylvania

Millersylvania was originally homesteaded by Squire Lathum in 1855 and later sold to the Miller family who called the property "Miller's Glade." Later the park was renamed Millersylvania meaning wooded glade. The family gave the property to the state in 1921 to be used as a park.

Millersylvania is a camping park complete with trails, swimming at Deep Lake and camping.

Mima Mounds NAP

Getting there

Near Little Rock, WA
Directions: From Littlerock, WA: Go West for .8 miles. Turn right on Waddell Creek Rd. Go .9 miles and turn left. Go 1 mile to the site.
Contact: (360)748.2383 or 753.1519, www.dnr.wa.gov/

Visitor information

Hours: Daily to dusk
Cost: The Discover Pass is required for motor-vehicle access to this area. (www.discoverpass.wa.gov)
Parking: See cost

Amenities:

* Interpretive center
* Nature trail

- Grassland
- Savannah
- Mima Mounds topography
- Woodland
- Restroom

About Mima Mounds NAP

Situated on glacial outwash left by the last Ice Age, Mima Mounds is located near Little Rock, WA and is a mysterious phenomenon. This natural area preserve was established in 1976 to preserve the rare landforms and Puget prairie grassland. This 445 acre preserve is open all year and offers about 5 miles of loop trails. An interpretive kiosk has information on the trails.

An unusual site, many theories have been formed on the origin of the large mounds including: gophers, Paul Bunyan, and seismic activity.

Nisqually National Wildlife Refuge

Getting there

Nisqually, WA
Directions: From I-5 take exit 114 to Nisqually, turn west and go under freeway and follow the signs to the refuge.
Contact: (360)753.1519, www.dnr.wa.gov/

Visitor information

Hours: Daily to dusk
Cost: There is a minimal fee per carload. Some passes are accepted here
Parking: See cost

Amenities

- 2,818 acre wildlife refuge
- 1 mile Twin Barns loop trail
- 5 mile Brown Farm loop trail
- Observation tower
- Salt marshes

About Nisqually National Wildlife Refuge

Once a farm, this refuge covers 2,818 acres offering two walking trails taking you through orchards and past the farmhouse. A 1 mile loop trail called Twin Barns is a boardwalk trail with access to an observation platform. The 5 mile loop called Brown Farm follows the Nisqually River and passes by flats and McAllister Creek. A two story viewing observation tower gives views of the saltwater tidal mudflats, birds, marshes and grasses.

Tolmie State Park

Getting there

7730 61st Ave NE, Olympia WA
Directions: Take exit #111 off I-5. Follow signs to park, approximately five miles.
Contact: (360)456.6464, www.parks.wa.gov

Visitor information

Hours: 8am to dusk
Cost: The Discover Pass is required for motor-vehicle access to state parks
(www.discoverpass.wa.gov)
Parking: Available in the upper or lower lot

Amenities

- 3 miles hiking trails
- Boating (saltwater)
- Diving
- Fishing
- Swimming
- Clamming

- Crabbing
- Beachcombing
- Bird Watching
- Wildlife Viewing

About Tolmie State Park:

Tolmie State park is named for Dr. William Frazer Tolmie. Tolmie spent 16 years with the Hudson Bay Company at Fort Nisqually as a physician, surgeon, botanist and fur trader.

105 acres of marine day-use park with saltwater shoreline on Nisqually Beach, Tolmie State Park offers beachside and underwater activities.

A kitchen at Tomie State Park

Two kitchen shelters are available by reservation by calling the park at 360-456-6464.

Western Chehalis Trail

Getting there

There are several locations to enter the trail between Olympia and Chehalis.

Directions: To Chambers Lake Trailhead: From I-5 northbound, take exit #108 to Sleater Kinney Road. Head south across Pacific Avenue at the 4 way stop sign turn right onto 14th Avenue. Follow approximately ½ mile. The entrance is after the trestle on the left.

Contact: (360)786.5595, www.co.thurston.wa.us

Visitor information

Hours: Daily to dusk
Cost: Free
Parking: Free parking

Amenities

- Walking trail
- Restroom
- Picnic areas

About Western Chehalis Trail

From 1926 through the mid 1980's, this trail was owned by Weyerhaeuser and was part of the Chehalis Western Railroad. The trail now runs north-south and links to the Yelm to Tenino Trail. It provides over 170 acres of park land, 2 miles of river access, Puget Sound access, Chambers Lake access, as well as access to forests, farms, creeks, prairies and wetlands. Mile markers every ½ mile run from Woodard Bay. The trail covers 22 miles, part owned by the Department of Natural Resources and part owned by Thurston County.

Chambers Lake Trailhead to Junction with Yelm-Tenino Trail = 14 miles
Chehalis Western trail & Yelm- Tenino Trail to Rainer = 2 miles
Chambers Lake to Rainer = 16 miles
Rainier to Yelm = 5 miles
Chehalis Western Trail & Yelm-Tenino Trail Junction to Tenino = 6.5 miles

See the Thurston County Parks web site for maps.

Yelm to Tenino Trail

Getting there

Near 105 Yelm Ave. Yelm, WA
Directions: Take the Tumwater exit off Highway 101. Cross over I-5, go past the Brewery and across Capitol Blvd to the light at Cleveland Avenue. At the light, turn right onto Yelm Hwy. Follow Yelm Hwy until it intersects with Highway 510 near the Nisqually Indian Reservation. At the intersection of Highway 510, turn right and follow into downtown Yelm. Turn right in front of Yelm City Hall. The trailhead parking area is to the right of City Hall.
Contact: (360)786.5595, www.co.thurston.wa.us

Visitor information

Hours: Daily to dusk
Cost: Free
Parking: Free parking

Amenities:

* 14.5 mile trail

About Yelm to Tenino Trail

Acquired by Thurston County from Burlington Northern Railroad in 1993, this 14.5 mile trail runs east-west connecting Yelm, Rainier and Tenino. The trail intersects the Western Chehalis Walking Trail. Mile markers are placed every ½ mile starting in Yelm.
Yelm to Rainer = 5 miles; Rainier to Chehalis Western Junction = 2 miles; Junction to Tenino = 6.5 miles

Part 5 - **Resources**

Individual entries have resources listed for contact information. The following resources are provided for you to expand on what is provided if you wish or can offer a quick reference if you need a web address or phone number. Many of the city websites also offer maps to the trails and parks that can be helpful – especially if you plan for a hike or to find a new route to a location.

Bigelow House
www.bigelowhouse.org

Columbus Park
5700 Black Lake Blvd SW #62
Olympia, WA 98515
360.786.9460
1.866.848.9460
www.columbuspark.net

Department of Natural Resources
360.577.2025
www.dnr.wa.gov

Evergreen State College
www.evergreen.edu

Access Washington
www.ga.wa.gov

Intercity Transit
www.intercitytransit.com

Lacey Parks and Recreation
www.ci.lacey.wa.us

NW Source
www.nwsource.com

Olympia Parks and Recreation
222 Columbia St. NW
Olympia, WA 98501
360.753.8380
olympiawa.gov

Skateboard Parks
www.skateboardparks.com

Thurston County Parks and Recreation
2617-A 12th Court SW
Olympia, WA 98502
360.786.5595
co.thurston.wa.us

Timberland Library
www.timberland.lib.wa.us

Tumwater Parks and Recreation
www.ci.tumwater.wa.us

Washington State History Museum
www.wshs.org

Contact the Author

Instagram
instagram.com/aregensburg

Facebook
facebook.com/ExploreOlympiaTumwaterLacey

Twitter
twitter.com/AngieLeaR

Made in the USA
San Bernardino, CA
20 July 2016